50 Sheet Pan Dinner Recipes for Home

By: Kelly Johnson

Table of Contents

- Sheet Pan Lemon Garlic Butter Shrimp with Asparagus
- Sheet Pan Balsamic Chicken with Roasted Vegetables
- Sheet Pan Teriyaki Salmon with Broccoli and Rice
- Sheet Pan Italian Sausage and Peppers with Potatoes
- Sheet Pan BBQ Ranch Chicken with Potatoes and Green Beans
- Sheet Pan Honey Mustard Pork Chops with Brussels Sprouts
- Sheet Pan Chili Lime Steak Fajitas with Bell Peppers and Onions
- Sheet Pan Lemon Herb Chicken with Roasted Potatoes and Carrots
- Sheet Pan Maple Dijon Salmon with Sweet Potatoes and Brussels Sprouts
- Sheet Pan Garlic Butter Steak and Shrimp with Asparagus
- Sheet Pan Pesto Chicken with Cherry Tomatoes and Zucchini
- Sheet Pan Greek Chicken with Roasted Vegetables and Tzatziki Sauce
- Sheet Pan Orange Glazed Pork Tenderloin with Broccoli and Carrots
- Sheet Pan Cajun Shrimp and Sausage with Potatoes and Corn
- Sheet Pan Moroccan Spiced Chicken with Cauliflower and Chickpeas
- Sheet Pan Honey Garlic Chicken with Bell Peppers and Snap Peas
- Sheet Pan Lemon Herb Tilapia with Asparagus and Potatoes
- Sheet Pan Hoisin Glazed Salmon with Bok Choy and Mushrooms
- Sheet Pan Buffalo Chicken with Sweet Potatoes and Green Beans
- Sheet Pan Rosemary Garlic Pork Chops with Brussels Sprouts and Apples
- Sheet Pan Coconut Lime Shrimp with Pineapple and Peppers
- Sheet Pan Mediterranean Chicken with Olives, Tomatoes, and Feta
- Sheet Pan Ranch Pork Chops with Potatoes and Broccoli
- Sheet Pan BBQ Chicken with Corn on the Cob and Potatoes
- Sheet Pan Chili Lime Cod with Bell Peppers and Onions
- Sheet Pan Maple Balsamic Chicken with Brussels Sprouts and Squash
- Sheet Pan Teriyaki Tofu with Broccoli and Bell Peppers
- Sheet Pan Lemon Pepper Chicken with Green Beans and Potatoes
- Sheet Pan Honey Sriracha Salmon with Snap Peas and Carrots
- Sheet Pan Caprese Chicken with Balsamic Glaze and Roasted Tomatoes
- Sheet Pan Mexican Street Corn Chicken with Potatoes and Peppers
- Sheet Pan Lemon Garlic Herb Tilapia with Asparagus and Tomatoes
- Sheet Pan Ginger Soy Glazed Salmon with Broccoli and Rice
- Sheet Pan Greek Lemon Chicken with Roasted Vegetables and Hummus
- Sheet Pan Garlic Butter Pork Chops with Brussels Sprouts and Potatoes

- Sheet Pan Honey Mustard Chicken with Brussels Sprouts and Carrots
- Sheet Pan Cajun Roasted Shrimp and Sausage with Peppers and Onions
- Sheet Pan Pesto Salmon with Asparagus and Cherry Tomatoes
- Sheet Pan BBQ Ranch Pork Tenderloin with Potatoes and Green Beans
- Sheet Pan Lemon Herb Tofu with Broccoli and Cauliflower
- Sheet Pan Moroccan Spiced Cod with Chickpeas and Bell Peppers
- Sheet Pan Teriyaki Chicken with Pineapple and Snap Peas
- Sheet Pan Italian Herb Chicken with Roasted Vegetables and Potatoes
- Sheet Pan Honey Garlic Glazed Pork Chops with Brussels Sprouts and Apples
- Sheet Pan Lemon Pepper Shrimp with Broccoli and Potatoes
- Sheet Pan Maple Dijon Chicken with Sweet Potatoes and Brussels Sprouts
- Sheet Pan BBQ Ranch Salmon with Corn on the Cob and Potatoes
- Sheet Pan Mediterranean Veggie Bowls with Chickpeas and Tzatziki
- Sheet Pan Teriyaki Beef and Broccoli with Rice
- Sheet Pan Honey Mustard Veggie Tofu with Potatoes and Green Beans

Sheet Pan Lemon Garlic Butter Shrimp with Asparagus

Ingredients:

- 1 pound large shrimp, peeled and deveined
- 1 pound asparagus, trimmed
- 4 cloves garlic, minced
- Zest of 1 lemon
- Juice of 1 lemon
- 4 tablespoons unsalted butter, melted
- 2 tablespoons olive oil
- Salt and black pepper, to taste
- Fresh parsley, chopped, for garnish

Instructions:

1. Preheat your oven to 400°F (200°C). Line a large baking sheet with parchment paper or aluminum foil.
2. In a small bowl, whisk together the minced garlic, lemon zest, lemon juice, melted butter, and olive oil to make the marinade.
3. Place the shrimp and trimmed asparagus on the prepared baking sheet. Pour the marinade over the shrimp and asparagus, making sure everything is evenly coated. Season with salt and black pepper to taste.
4. Arrange the shrimp and asparagus in a single layer on the baking sheet, making sure they are not overcrowded.
5. Roast in the preheated oven for 10-12 minutes, or until the shrimp are pink and opaque and the asparagus is tender-crisp.
6. Remove the baking sheet from the oven and garnish the shrimp and asparagus with chopped fresh parsley.
7. Serve the Sheet Pan Lemon Garlic Butter Shrimp with Asparagus immediately, either on its own or over cooked rice, pasta, or quinoa.
8. Enjoy your delicious and flavorful meal!

This dish is perfect for a quick and healthy weeknight dinner or a special occasion meal.

It's sure to become a favorite in your household!

Sheet Pan Balsamic Chicken with Roasted Vegetables

Ingredients:

For the balsamic chicken:

- 4 boneless, skinless chicken breasts
- 1/4 cup balsamic vinegar
- 2 tablespoons olive oil
- 2 cloves garlic, minced
- 1 teaspoon dried thyme
- 1 teaspoon dried rosemary
- Salt and black pepper, to taste

For the roasted vegetables:

- 1 pound baby potatoes, halved
- 2 bell peppers, chopped (any color)
- 1 red onion, chopped
- 1 zucchini, sliced
- 1 tablespoon olive oil
- Salt and black pepper, to taste
- 2 tablespoons balsamic vinegar (optional, for drizzling)

Instructions:

1. Preheat your oven to 400°F (200°C). Line a large baking sheet with parchment paper or aluminum foil for easy cleanup.
2. In a small bowl, whisk together the balsamic vinegar, olive oil, minced garlic, dried thyme, dried rosemary, salt, and black pepper to make the marinade for the chicken.
3. Place the chicken breasts in a shallow dish or resealable plastic bag. Pour the marinade over the chicken, making sure it's evenly coated. Let the chicken marinate in the refrigerator for at least 30 minutes, or up to 4 hours for maximum flavor.

4. In a separate large bowl, toss together the halved baby potatoes, chopped bell peppers, chopped red onion, and sliced zucchini with olive oil, salt, and black pepper.
5. Spread the marinated chicken breasts and the seasoned vegetables in a single layer on the prepared baking sheet, making sure they are not overcrowded.
6. Roast in the preheated oven for 20-25 minutes, or until the chicken is cooked through (internal temperature of 165°F/75°C) and the vegetables are tender and golden brown.
7. If desired, drizzle the roasted vegetables with additional balsamic vinegar for extra flavor before serving.
8. Serve the Sheet Pan Balsamic Chicken with Roasted Vegetables hot, garnished with chopped fresh herbs if desired.

Enjoy your delicious and nutritious meal!

Sheet Pan Teriyaki Salmon with Broccoli and Rice

Ingredients:

For the teriyaki salmon:

- 4 salmon fillets
- 1/4 cup soy sauce
- 2 tablespoons honey
- 1 tablespoon rice vinegar
- 1 tablespoon sesame oil
- 2 cloves garlic, minced
- 1 teaspoon grated ginger
- Sesame seeds, for garnish
- Sliced green onions, for garnish

For the broccoli and rice:

- 2 cups broccoli florets
- 1 cup uncooked rice
- 2 cups water or chicken broth
- Salt, to taste
- Black pepper, to taste

Instructions:

1. Preheat your oven to 400°F (200°C). Line a large baking sheet with parchment paper or aluminum foil for easy cleanup.
2. In a small bowl, whisk together the soy sauce, honey, rice vinegar, sesame oil, minced garlic, and grated ginger to make the teriyaki sauce.
3. Place the salmon fillets in a shallow dish or resealable plastic bag. Pour the teriyaki sauce over the salmon, making sure it's evenly coated. Let the salmon marinate in the refrigerator for at least 30 minutes, or up to 1 hour for maximum flavor.

4. In a separate bowl, toss the broccoli florets with olive oil, salt, and black pepper until evenly coated.
5. Spread the marinated salmon fillets and the seasoned broccoli florets on the prepared baking sheet, making sure they are not overcrowded.
6. In a saucepan, combine the uncooked rice with water or chicken broth. Bring to a boil, then reduce the heat to low, cover, and simmer for 15-20 minutes, or until the rice is cooked and the liquid is absorbed.
7. Place the baking sheet with the salmon and broccoli in the preheated oven. Roast for 12-15 minutes, or until the salmon is cooked through and flakes easily with a fork, and the broccoli is tender and slightly crispy around the edges.
8. While the salmon and broccoli are cooking, fluff the cooked rice with a fork.
9. Remove the baking sheet from the oven. Sprinkle the salmon fillets with sesame seeds and sliced green onions for garnish.
10. Serve the Sheet Pan Teriyaki Salmon with Broccoli and Rice hot, with the cooked rice on the side.

Enjoy your delicious and satisfying meal!

Sheet Pan Italian Sausage and Peppers with Potatoes

Ingredients:

- 1 pound Italian sausage links (mild or spicy), sliced
- 1 red bell pepper, sliced
- 1 green bell pepper, sliced
- 1 yellow onion, sliced
- 1 pound baby potatoes, halved
- 2 tablespoons olive oil
- 2 cloves garlic, minced
- 1 teaspoon dried oregano
- 1 teaspoon dried basil
- Salt and black pepper, to taste
- Fresh parsley, chopped, for garnish

Instructions:

1. Preheat your oven to 400°F (200°C). Line a large baking sheet with parchment paper or aluminum foil for easy cleanup.
2. In a large bowl, toss together the sliced Italian sausage, sliced bell peppers, sliced onion, halved baby potatoes, olive oil, minced garlic, dried oregano, dried basil, salt, and black pepper until evenly coated.
3. Spread the sausage, peppers, onions, and potatoes in a single layer on the prepared baking sheet, making sure they are not overcrowded.
4. Roast in the preheated oven for 25-30 minutes, or until the sausage is cooked through, the peppers and onions are tender, and the potatoes are golden brown and crispy on the edges. Stir halfway through cooking to ensure even cooking.
5. Remove the baking sheet from the oven and garnish the Italian sausage and peppers with chopped fresh parsley for a pop of color and flavor.
6. Serve the Sheet Pan Italian Sausage and Peppers with Potatoes hot, straight from the oven.

Enjoy your delicious and satisfying meal!

Sheet Pan BBQ Ranch Chicken with Potatoes and Green Beans

Ingredients:

- 4 boneless, skinless chicken breasts
- 1 pound baby potatoes, halved or quartered
- 1 pound fresh green beans, trimmed
- 1/2 cup BBQ sauce
- 1/4 cup ranch dressing
- 2 tablespoons olive oil
- 2 cloves garlic, minced
- Salt and black pepper, to taste
- Fresh parsley, chopped, for garnish (optional)

Instructions:

1. Preheat your oven to 400°F (200°C). Line a large baking sheet with parchment paper or aluminum foil for easy cleanup.
2. In a small bowl, whisk together the BBQ sauce, ranch dressing, olive oil, minced garlic, salt, and black pepper to make the marinade.
3. Place the chicken breasts in a shallow dish or resealable plastic bag. Pour half of the marinade over the chicken, reserving the remaining half for later. Let the chicken marinate in the refrigerator for at least 30 minutes, or up to 4 hours for maximum flavor.
4. In a large bowl, toss together the halved baby potatoes and trimmed green beans with olive oil, salt, and black pepper until evenly coated.
5. Spread the marinated chicken breasts, halved baby potatoes, and trimmed green beans in a single layer on the prepared baking sheet, making sure they are not overcrowded.
6. Roast in the preheated oven for 25-30 minutes, or until the chicken is cooked through (internal temperature of 165°F/75°C), the potatoes are golden brown and crispy on the edges, and the green beans are tender-crisp.
7. During the last 10 minutes of cooking, brush the reserved marinade over the chicken, potatoes, and green beans, allowing it to caramelize slightly.
8. Remove the baking sheet from the oven and garnish the Sheet Pan BBQ Ranch Chicken with Potatoes and Green Beans with chopped fresh parsley for a pop of color and freshness, if desired.

9. Serve hot and enjoy your delicious and satisfying meal!

This dish is sure to be a hit with the whole family, and it's easy to customize with your favorite BBQ sauce and ranch dressing flavors.

Sheet Pan Honey Mustard Pork Chops with Brussels Sprouts

Ingredients:

- 4 bone-in pork chops
- 1 pound Brussels sprouts, trimmed and halved
- 2 tablespoons olive oil
- Salt and black pepper, to taste
- 1/4 cup honey
- 2 tablespoons Dijon mustard
- 2 cloves garlic, minced
- 1 tablespoon apple cider vinegar
- 1 tablespoon soy sauce
- 1 teaspoon dried thyme
- 1 teaspoon paprika
- Fresh parsley, chopped, for garnish (optional)

Instructions:

1. Preheat your oven to 400°F (200°C). Line a large baking sheet with parchment paper or aluminum foil for easy cleanup.
2. Season the pork chops with salt and black pepper on both sides.
3. In a small bowl, whisk together the honey, Dijon mustard, minced garlic, apple cider vinegar, soy sauce, dried thyme, and paprika to make the honey mustard glaze.
4. Place the trimmed and halved Brussels sprouts on the prepared baking sheet. Drizzle with olive oil, season with salt and black pepper, and toss to coat evenly.
5. Push the Brussels sprouts to the sides of the baking sheet to make room for the pork chops in the center.
6. Arrange the seasoned pork chops in the center of the baking sheet.
7. Brush the honey mustard glaze over the pork chops, coating them evenly on both sides.
8. Roast in the preheated oven for 20-25 minutes, or until the pork chops are cooked through (internal temperature of 145°F/63°C) and the Brussels sprouts are tender and caramelized.
9. If desired, broil for an additional 2-3 minutes at the end of cooking to brown the pork chops and Brussels sprouts slightly.

10. Remove the baking sheet from the oven and let the Sheet Pan Honey Mustard Pork Chops with Brussels Sprouts rest for a few minutes.
11. Garnish with chopped fresh parsley for a pop of color and freshness before serving, if desired.
12. Serve hot and enjoy your delicious and flavorful meal!

This dish is perfect for a weeknight dinner or a special occasion, and it's sure to impress with its savory-sweet flavor combination.

Sheet Pan Chili Lime Steak Fajitas with Bell Peppers and Onions

Ingredients:

- 1 ½ pounds flank steak, thinly sliced against the grain
- 3 bell peppers (red, green, and yellow), thinly sliced
- 1 large onion, thinly sliced
- 3 tablespoons olive oil
- 3 tablespoons freshly squeezed lime juice
- Zest of 1 lime
- 2 cloves garlic, minced
- 1 tablespoon chili powder
- 1 teaspoon ground cumin
- 1 teaspoon smoked paprika
- 1 teaspoon dried oregano
- 1 teaspoon salt, or to taste
- ½ teaspoon black pepper, or to taste
- 8 small flour tortillas, warmed
- Optional toppings: sliced avocado, sour cream, shredded cheese, chopped cilantro, lime wedges

Instructions:

1. Preheat your oven to 400°F (200°C). Line a large baking sheet with parchment paper or aluminum foil for easy cleanup.
2. In a large bowl, combine the sliced flank steak, bell peppers, and onion.
3. In a small bowl, whisk together the olive oil, lime juice, lime zest, minced garlic, chili powder, ground cumin, smoked paprika, dried oregano, salt, and black pepper.
4. Pour the marinade over the steak and vegetable mixture. Toss until everything is evenly coated.
5. Spread the steak and vegetables in a single layer on the prepared baking sheet.
6. Roast in the preheated oven for 15-20 minutes, or until the steak is cooked to your desired level of doneness and the vegetables are tender and slightly caramelized.
7. While the steak and vegetables are cooking, warm the flour tortillas in a dry skillet or in the oven.

8. Once done, remove the baking sheet from the oven and let it cool for a few minutes.
9. Serve the chili lime steak fajitas with warm tortillas and optional toppings such as sliced avocado, sour cream, shredded cheese, chopped cilantro, and lime wedges.
10. Enjoy your delicious and flavorful meal!

These sheet pan chili lime steak fajitas are perfect for a family dinner or a casual get-together with friends. They're easy to make and packed with vibrant flavors!

Sheet Pan Lemon Herb Chicken with Roasted Potatoes and Carrots

Ingredients:

For the lemon herb chicken:

- 4 bone-in, skin-on chicken thighs
- 2 tablespoons olive oil
- Zest of 1 lemon
- Juice of 1 lemon
- 2 cloves garlic, minced
- 1 teaspoon dried thyme
- 1 teaspoon dried rosemary
- Salt and black pepper, to taste

For the roasted potatoes and carrots:

- 1 pound baby potatoes, halved
- 1 pound carrots, peeled and sliced into sticks
- 2 tablespoons olive oil
- Salt and black pepper, to taste
- 1 teaspoon dried thyme
- 1 teaspoon dried rosemary
- 1 teaspoon paprika

Instructions:

1. Preheat your oven to 400°F (200°C). Line a large baking sheet with parchment paper or aluminum foil for easy cleanup.
2. In a small bowl, whisk together the olive oil, lemon zest, lemon juice, minced garlic, dried thyme, dried rosemary, salt, and black pepper to make the marinade for the chicken.
3. Place the chicken thighs in a shallow dish or resealable plastic bag. Pour the marinade over the chicken, making sure it's evenly coated. Let the chicken

marinate in the refrigerator for at least 30 minutes, or up to 4 hours for maximum flavor.
4. In a large bowl, toss together the halved baby potatoes and sliced carrots with olive oil, salt, black pepper, dried thyme, dried rosemary, and paprika until evenly coated.
5. Spread the marinated chicken thighs, halved baby potatoes, and sliced carrots in a single layer on the prepared baking sheet, making sure they are not overcrowded.
6. Roast in the preheated oven for 30-35 minutes, or until the chicken is cooked through (internal temperature of 165°F/75°C) and the potatoes and carrots are tender and golden brown.
7. If desired, broil for an additional 2-3 minutes at the end of cooking to brown the chicken and vegetables slightly.
8. Remove the baking sheet from the oven and let the Sheet Pan Lemon Herb Chicken with Roasted Potatoes and Carrots rest for a few minutes before serving.
9. Serve hot and enjoy your delicious and flavorful meal!

This dish is perfect for a family dinner or a casual gathering, and it's sure to be a hit with its bright lemony flavor and savory herbs.

Sheet Pan Maple Dijon Salmon with Sweet Potatoes and Brussels Sprouts

Ingredients:

For the maple Dijon salmon:

- 4 salmon fillets
- 3 tablespoons maple syrup
- 2 tablespoons Dijon mustard
- 1 tablespoon soy sauce
- 1 tablespoon olive oil
- 2 cloves garlic, minced
- Salt and black pepper, to taste

For the sweet potatoes and Brussels sprouts:

- 2 large sweet potatoes, peeled and cut into cubes
- 1 pound Brussels sprouts, trimmed and halved
- 2 tablespoons olive oil
- Salt and black pepper, to taste
- 1 teaspoon garlic powder
- 1 teaspoon paprika

Instructions:

1. Preheat your oven to 400°F (200°C). Line a large baking sheet with parchment paper or aluminum foil for easy cleanup.
2. In a small bowl, whisk together the maple syrup, Dijon mustard, soy sauce, olive oil, minced garlic, salt, and black pepper to make the marinade for the salmon.
3. Place the salmon fillets in a shallow dish or resealable plastic bag. Pour the marinade over the salmon, making sure it's evenly coated. Let the salmon marinate in the refrigerator for at least 30 minutes, or up to 4 hours for maximum flavor.

4. In a large bowl, toss together the cubed sweet potatoes and halved Brussels sprouts with olive oil, salt, black pepper, garlic powder, and paprika until evenly coated.
5. Spread the marinated salmon fillets, cubed sweet potatoes, and halved Brussels sprouts in a single layer on the prepared baking sheet, making sure they are not overcrowded.
6. Roast in the preheated oven for 20-25 minutes, or until the salmon is cooked through (internal temperature of 145°F/63°C) and flakes easily with a fork, and the sweet potatoes and Brussels sprouts are tender and caramelized.
7. If desired, broil for an additional 2-3 minutes at the end of cooking to brown the salmon and vegetables slightly.
8. Remove the baking sheet from the oven and let the Sheet Pan Maple Dijon Salmon with Sweet Potatoes and Brussels Sprouts rest for a few minutes before serving.
9. Serve hot and enjoy your delicious and nutritious meal!

This dish is perfect for a family dinner or a special occasion, and it's sure to impress with its sweet and savory flavors.

Sheet Pan Garlic Butter Steak and Shrimp with Asparagus

Ingredients:

For the garlic butter:

- 1/2 cup unsalted butter, melted
- 4 cloves garlic, minced
- 2 tablespoons fresh parsley, chopped
- Salt and black pepper, to taste

For the steak and shrimp:

- 1 pound steak (such as sirloin or ribeye), cut into cubes
- 1 pound large shrimp, peeled and deveined
- 1 bunch asparagus, trimmed
- Salt and black pepper, to taste
- 2 tablespoons olive oil

Instructions:

1. Preheat your oven to 400°F (200°C). Line a large baking sheet with parchment paper or aluminum foil for easy cleanup.
2. In a small bowl, whisk together the melted butter, minced garlic, chopped parsley, salt, and black pepper to make the garlic butter.
3. Place the cubed steak and peeled and deveined shrimp in a large bowl. Pour half of the garlic butter over the steak and shrimp, reserving the remaining half for later. Toss until the steak and shrimp are evenly coated.
4. Arrange the seasoned steak and shrimp on one side of the prepared baking sheet.
5. Place the trimmed asparagus on the other side of the baking sheet. Drizzle with olive oil and season with salt and black pepper to taste.
6. Roast in the preheated oven for 10-12 minutes, or until the steak is cooked to your desired level of doneness, the shrimp are pink and opaque, and the asparagus is tender-crisp.
7. During the last few minutes of cooking, brush the reserved garlic butter over the steak, shrimp, and asparagus.

8. Remove the baking sheet from the oven and let it cool for a few minutes before serving.
9. Serve the Sheet Pan Garlic Butter Steak and Shrimp with Asparagus hot, garnished with additional chopped parsley if desired.
10. Enjoy your delicious and flavorful meal!

This dish is perfect for a special occasion or a weeknight dinner, and it's sure to impress with its juicy steak, succulent shrimp, and tender-crisp asparagus, all coated in flavorful garlic butter.

Sheet Pan Pesto Chicken with Cherry Tomatoes and Zucchini

Ingredients:

- 4 boneless, skinless chicken breasts
- 1/2 cup basil pesto (store-bought or homemade)
- 1 pint cherry tomatoes, halved
- 2 medium zucchini, sliced
- 2 tablespoons olive oil
- Salt and black pepper, to taste
- Grated Parmesan cheese, for serving (optional)
- Fresh basil leaves, chopped, for garnish (optional)

Instructions:

1. Preheat your oven to 400°F (200°C). Line a large baking sheet with parchment paper or aluminum foil for easy cleanup.
2. Place the chicken breasts on the prepared baking sheet. Season both sides of the chicken breasts with salt and black pepper to taste.
3. Spread a generous amount of basil pesto evenly over each chicken breast, covering the top surface.
4. In a large bowl, toss the halved cherry tomatoes and sliced zucchini with olive oil, salt, and black pepper until evenly coated.
5. Arrange the cherry tomatoes and zucchini around the chicken breasts on the baking sheet, ensuring everything is in a single layer.
6. Roast in the preheated oven for 20-25 minutes, or until the chicken is cooked through (internal temperature of 165°F/75°C) and the vegetables are tender.
7. Optional: During the last few minutes of cooking, sprinkle grated Parmesan cheese over the chicken and vegetables, if desired, and return the baking sheet to the oven until the cheese is melted and bubbly.
8. Remove the baking sheet from the oven and let it cool for a few minutes.
9. Serve the Sheet Pan Pesto Chicken with Cherry Tomatoes and Zucchini hot, garnished with chopped fresh basil leaves for extra flavor.
10. Enjoy your delicious and flavorful meal!

This dish is perfect for a quick and healthy weeknight dinner, and it's sure to become a family favorite with its vibrant colors and delightful pesto flavor.

Sheet Pan Greek Chicken with Roasted Vegetables and Tzatziki Sauce

Ingredients:

For the Greek chicken:

- 4 boneless, skinless chicken breasts
- 2 tablespoons olive oil
- 2 cloves garlic, minced
- 1 teaspoon dried oregano
- 1 teaspoon dried thyme
- 1 teaspoon dried rosemary
- Salt and black pepper, to taste
- Juice of 1 lemon

For the roasted vegetables:

- 1 large red bell pepper, sliced
- 1 large yellow bell pepper, sliced
- 1 red onion, sliced
- 1 pint cherry tomatoes
- 1 tablespoon olive oil
- Salt and black pepper, to taste
- 1 teaspoon dried oregano
- 1 teaspoon dried thyme
- 1 teaspoon dried rosemary

For the tzatziki sauce:

- 1 cup Greek yogurt
- 1 cucumber, grated and squeezed to remove excess moisture
- 2 cloves garlic, minced
- 1 tablespoon lemon juice
- 1 tablespoon chopped fresh dill (or 1 teaspoon dried dill)
- Salt and black pepper, to taste

Instructions:

1. Preheat your oven to 400°F (200°C). Line a large baking sheet with parchment paper or aluminum foil for easy cleanup.
2. In a small bowl, whisk together the olive oil, minced garlic, dried oregano, dried thyme, dried rosemary, salt, black pepper, and lemon juice to make the marinade for the chicken.
3. Place the chicken breasts in a shallow dish or resealable plastic bag. Pour the marinade over the chicken, making sure it's evenly coated. Let the chicken marinate in the refrigerator for at least 30 minutes, or up to 4 hours for maximum flavor.
4. In a large bowl, toss together the sliced bell peppers, sliced red onion, cherry tomatoes, olive oil, salt, black pepper, dried oregano, dried thyme, and dried rosemary until evenly coated.
5. Spread the marinated chicken breasts and the seasoned vegetables in a single layer on the prepared baking sheet, making sure they are not overcrowded.
6. Roast in the preheated oven for 25-30 minutes, or until the chicken is cooked through (internal temperature of 165°F/75°C) and the vegetables are tender and slightly caramelized.
7. While the chicken and vegetables are roasting, prepare the tzatziki sauce. In a medium bowl, combine the Greek yogurt, grated cucumber, minced garlic, lemon juice, chopped fresh dill, salt, and black pepper. Stir until well combined. Taste and adjust seasoning, if needed.
8. Remove the baking sheet from the oven and let it cool for a few minutes.
9. Serve the Sheet Pan Greek Chicken with Roasted Vegetables hot, with a dollop of tzatziki sauce on top.
10. Enjoy your delicious and flavorful meal!

This dish is perfect for a family dinner or a special occasion, and it's sure to impress with its Greek-inspired flavors and vibrant colors.

Sheet Pan Orange Glazed Pork Tenderloin with Broccoli and Carrots

Ingredients:

For the orange glazed pork tenderloin:

- 2 pork tenderloins (about 1 pound each)
- Zest and juice of 2 oranges
- 1/4 cup soy sauce
- 2 tablespoons honey
- 2 tablespoons olive oil
- 2 cloves garlic, minced
- 1 teaspoon ground ginger
- Salt and black pepper, to taste
- Crushed red pepper flakes, to taste (optional)

For the broccoli and carrots:

- 1 head of broccoli, cut into florets
- 2 large carrots, peeled and sliced into sticks
- 2 tablespoons olive oil
- Salt and black pepper, to taste
- 1 teaspoon garlic powder
- 1 teaspoon paprika

Instructions:

1. Preheat your oven to 400°F (200°C). Line a large baking sheet with parchment paper or aluminum foil for easy cleanup.
2. In a small bowl, whisk together the orange zest, orange juice, soy sauce, honey, olive oil, minced garlic, ground ginger, salt, black pepper, and crushed red pepper flakes (if using) to make the marinade for the pork tenderloin.
3. Place the pork tenderloins in a shallow dish or resealable plastic bag. Pour the marinade over the pork tenderloins, making sure they are evenly coated. Let them

marinate in the refrigerator for at least 30 minutes, or up to 4 hours for maximum flavor.
4. In a large bowl, toss together the broccoli florets and sliced carrots with olive oil, salt, black pepper, garlic powder, and paprika until evenly coated.
5. Spread the marinated pork tenderloins and seasoned broccoli and carrots in a single layer on the prepared baking sheet, making sure they are not overcrowded.
6. Roast in the preheated oven for 20-25 minutes, or until the pork tenderloins reach an internal temperature of 145°F (63°C) and the vegetables are tender-crisp.
7. If desired, broil for an additional 2-3 minutes at the end of cooking to brown the pork tenderloins and vegetables slightly.
8. Remove the baking sheet from the oven and let it cool for a few minutes.
9. Slice the pork tenderloins into medallions and serve them with the roasted broccoli and carrots.
10. Enjoy your delicious and flavorful Sheet Pan Orange Glazed Pork Tenderloin with Broccoli and Carrots!

This dish is sure to be a hit with its sweet and tangy orange glaze and tender-crisp vegetables. It's perfect for a healthy and satisfying meal any night of the week.

Sheet Pan Cajun Shrimp and Sausage with Potatoes and Corn

Ingredients:

- 1 pound large shrimp, peeled and deveined
- 1 pound smoked sausage, sliced into rounds
- 1 pound baby potatoes, halved
- 2 ears of corn, husked and cut into thirds
- 2 tablespoons olive oil
- 2 tablespoons Cajun seasoning
- 1 teaspoon paprika
- 1 teaspoon garlic powder
- 1 teaspoon onion powder
- Salt and black pepper, to taste
- Fresh parsley, chopped, for garnish (optional)
- Lemon wedges, for serving (optional)

Instructions:

1. Preheat your oven to 400°F (200°C). Line a large baking sheet with parchment paper or aluminum foil for easy cleanup.
2. In a large bowl, combine the shrimp, sliced smoked sausage, halved baby potatoes, and corn pieces.
3. Drizzle olive oil over the shrimp, sausage, potatoes, and corn, tossing to coat evenly.
4. In a small bowl, mix together the Cajun seasoning, paprika, garlic powder, onion powder, salt, and black pepper.
5. Sprinkle the Cajun seasoning mixture over the shrimp, sausage, potatoes, and corn, tossing to coat evenly.
6. Spread the shrimp, sausage, potatoes, and corn in a single layer on the prepared baking sheet.
7. Roast in the preheated oven for 20-25 minutes, or until the shrimp are pink and cooked through, the sausage is browned and crispy on the edges, and the potatoes are tender.
8. Remove the baking sheet from the oven and let it cool for a few minutes.
9. Garnish with chopped fresh parsley, if desired, and serve hot with lemon wedges on the side for squeezing over the shrimp, sausage, potatoes, and corn.

10. Enjoy your delicious and flavorful Sheet Pan Cajun Shrimp and Sausage with Potatoes and Corn!

This dish is sure to be a hit with its bold Cajun flavors and comforting combination of shrimp, sausage, potatoes, and corn. It's perfect for a fuss-free and satisfying meal any night of the week.

Sheet Pan Moroccan Spiced Chicken with Cauliflower and Chickpeas

Ingredients:

For the Moroccan spice blend:

- 2 teaspoons ground cumin
- 2 teaspoons ground coriander
- 1 teaspoon ground paprika
- 1 teaspoon ground turmeric
- 1/2 teaspoon ground cinnamon
- 1/2 teaspoon ground ginger
- 1/4 teaspoon cayenne pepper (adjust to taste)
- Salt and black pepper, to taste

For the chicken and vegetables:

- 4 bone-in, skin-on chicken thighs
- 1 head cauliflower, cut into florets
- 1 can (15 ounces) chickpeas, drained and rinsed
- 2 tablespoons olive oil
- Juice of 1 lemon
- 4 cloves garlic, minced
- Fresh cilantro, chopped, for garnish (optional)
- Lemon wedges, for serving

Instructions:

1. Preheat your oven to 400°F (200°C). Line a large baking sheet with parchment paper or aluminum foil for easy cleanup.
2. In a small bowl, mix together the Moroccan spice blend ingredients: ground cumin, ground coriander, ground paprika, ground turmeric, ground cinnamon, ground ginger, cayenne pepper, salt, and black pepper. Set aside.

3. Pat the chicken thighs dry with paper towels. Rub the chicken thighs with 1 tablespoon of olive oil and half of the Moroccan spice blend, coating them evenly.
4. In a large bowl, toss the cauliflower florets and chickpeas with the remaining 1 tablespoon of olive oil, minced garlic, lemon juice, and the rest of the Moroccan spice blend until evenly coated.
5. Spread the seasoned cauliflower florets and chickpeas on the prepared baking sheet, making an even layer. Arrange the chicken thighs on top of the vegetables.
6. Roast in the preheated oven for 30-35 minutes, or until the chicken is cooked through (internal temperature of 165°F/75°C) and the cauliflower is tender, with crispy edges.
7. Remove the baking sheet from the oven and let it cool for a few minutes.
8. Garnish with chopped fresh cilantro, if desired, and serve hot with lemon wedges on the side.
9. Enjoy your delicious and aromatic Sheet Pan Moroccan Spiced Chicken with Cauliflower and Chickpeas!

This dish is perfect for a flavorful and satisfying meal any night of the week. The Moroccan spices add depth of flavor to the chicken, cauliflower, and chickpeas, making it a delightful and comforting dish to enjoy with your family or friends.

Sheet Pan Honey Garlic Chicken with Bell Peppers and Snap Peas

Ingredients:

For the honey garlic sauce:

- 1/4 cup honey
- 3 tablespoons soy sauce
- 2 tablespoons olive oil
- 4 cloves garlic, minced
- 1 tablespoon rice vinegar
- 1 teaspoon sesame oil
- 1 teaspoon cornstarch (optional, for thickening)

For the chicken and vegetables:

- 4 boneless, skinless chicken breasts, cut into bite-sized pieces
- 2 bell peppers, thinly sliced (use a mix of colors for variety)
- 1 cup snap peas, trimmed
- 2 tablespoons olive oil
- Salt and black pepper, to taste
- Sesame seeds, for garnish (optional)
- Chopped green onions, for garnish (optional)

Instructions:

1. Preheat your oven to 400°F (200°C). Line a large baking sheet with parchment paper or aluminum foil for easy cleanup.
2. In a small saucepan, combine the honey, soy sauce, olive oil, minced garlic, rice vinegar, and sesame oil. Heat over medium heat, stirring constantly, until the mixture comes to a simmer.
3. Optional: In a small bowl, mix the cornstarch with 1 tablespoon of water to make a slurry. Stir the slurry into the sauce and continue cooking until the sauce thickens slightly. Remove from heat and set aside.

4. In a large bowl, combine the chicken pieces, sliced bell peppers, and snap peas. Drizzle with olive oil and season with salt and black pepper. Toss until everything is evenly coated.
5. Spread the chicken and vegetables in a single layer on the prepared baking sheet.
6. Pour the honey garlic sauce over the chicken and vegetables, using a spoon to coat them evenly.
7. Roast in the preheated oven for 20-25 minutes, or until the chicken is cooked through and the vegetables are tender-crisp.
8. If desired, garnish with sesame seeds and chopped green onions before serving.
9. Serve hot and enjoy your delicious Sheet Pan Honey Garlic Chicken with Bell Peppers and Snap Peas!

This dish is perfect for a quick and healthy weeknight dinner. The sweet and savory honey garlic sauce adds fantastic flavor to the tender chicken and crisp-tender vegetables, making it a surefire crowd-pleaser.

Sheet Pan Lemon Herb Tilapia with Asparagus and Potatoes

Ingredients:

- 4 tilapia fillets
- 1 pound asparagus, trimmed
- 1 pound baby potatoes, halved
- 2 tablespoons olive oil
- Zest and juice of 1 lemon
- 2 cloves garlic, minced
- 1 teaspoon dried thyme
- 1 teaspoon dried rosemary
- Salt and black pepper, to taste
- Fresh parsley, chopped, for garnish (optional)

Instructions:

1. Preheat your oven to 400°F (200°C). Line a large baking sheet with parchment paper or aluminum foil for easy cleanup.
2. In a small bowl, whisk together the olive oil, lemon zest, lemon juice, minced garlic, dried thyme, dried rosemary, salt, and black pepper to make the marinade.
3. Place the tilapia fillets, trimmed asparagus, and halved baby potatoes in a single layer on the prepared baking sheet.
4. Drizzle the marinade over the tilapia, asparagus, and potatoes, making sure they are evenly coated.
5. Toss the vegetables and tilapia gently to coat them in the marinade.
6. Season the vegetables and tilapia with additional salt and black pepper, if desired.
7. Roast in the preheated oven for 15-20 minutes, or until the tilapia is cooked through and flakes easily with a fork, and the vegetables are tender.
8. Remove the baking sheet from the oven and let it cool for a few minutes.
9. Garnish with chopped fresh parsley, if desired, before serving.
10. Serve hot and enjoy your delicious Sheet Pan Lemon Herb Tilapia with Asparagus and Potatoes!

This dish is light, flavorful, and easy to customize with your favorite herbs and spices.

It's perfect for a healthy weeknight dinner or a quick meal prep option.

Sheet Pan Hoisin Glazed Salmon with Bok Choy and Mushrooms

Ingredients:

For the hoisin glaze:

- 1/4 cup hoisin sauce
- 2 tablespoons soy sauce
- 1 tablespoon rice vinegar
- 1 tablespoon honey
- 2 cloves garlic, minced
- 1 teaspoon grated ginger
- 1 teaspoon sesame oil

For the salmon and vegetables:

- 4 salmon fillets
- 4 baby bok choy, halved lengthwise
- 8 ounces mushrooms, sliced
- 2 tablespoons olive oil
- Salt and black pepper, to taste
- Sesame seeds, for garnish (optional)
- Sliced green onions, for garnish (optional)

Instructions:

1. Preheat your oven to 400°F (200°C). Line a large baking sheet with parchment paper or aluminum foil for easy cleanup.
2. In a small bowl, whisk together the hoisin sauce, soy sauce, rice vinegar, honey, minced garlic, grated ginger, and sesame oil to make the hoisin glaze. Set aside.
3. Place the salmon fillets on the prepared baking sheet. Brush each fillet generously with the hoisin glaze, reserving some glaze for later.
4. In a large bowl, toss the halved baby bok choy and sliced mushrooms with olive oil, salt, and black pepper until evenly coated.

5. Arrange the seasoned bok choy and mushrooms around the salmon fillets on the baking sheet.
6. Roast in the preheated oven for 12-15 minutes, or until the salmon is cooked through and flakes easily with a fork, and the bok choy and mushrooms are tender.
7. During the last few minutes of cooking, brush the reserved hoisin glaze over the salmon fillets for extra flavor.
8. Remove the baking sheet from the oven and let it cool for a few minutes.
9. Optional: Garnish with sesame seeds and sliced green onions before serving.
10. Serve hot and enjoy your delicious Sheet Pan Hoisin Glazed Salmon with Bok Choy and Mushrooms!

This dish is perfect for a quick and healthy weeknight dinner. The hoisin glaze adds a delightful sweet and savory flavor to the salmon, while the bok choy and mushrooms provide a nutritious and tasty side.

Sheet Pan Buffalo Chicken with Sweet Potatoes and Green Beans

Ingredients:

For the buffalo chicken:

- 4 boneless, skinless chicken breasts
- 1/2 cup buffalo sauce
- 2 tablespoons olive oil
- 2 cloves garlic, minced
- 1 teaspoon paprika
- 1/2 teaspoon onion powder
- Salt and black pepper, to taste

For the sweet potatoes and green beans:

- 2 large sweet potatoes, peeled and cut into cubes
- 1 pound green beans, trimmed
- 2 tablespoons olive oil
- Salt and black pepper, to taste
- 1 teaspoon garlic powder
- 1 teaspoon dried thyme

Instructions:

1. Preheat your oven to 400°F (200°C). Line a large baking sheet with parchment paper or aluminum foil for easy cleanup.
2. In a small bowl, whisk together the buffalo sauce, olive oil, minced garlic, paprika, onion powder, salt, and black pepper to make the marinade for the chicken.
3. Place the chicken breasts in a shallow dish or resealable plastic bag. Pour the buffalo sauce marinade over the chicken, making sure it's evenly coated. Let the chicken marinate in the refrigerator for at least 30 minutes.
4. In a large bowl, toss together the cubed sweet potatoes and trimmed green beans with olive oil, salt, black pepper, garlic powder, and dried thyme until evenly coated.

5. Spread the marinated chicken breasts, cubed sweet potatoes, and green beans in a single layer on the prepared baking sheet, making sure they are not overcrowded.
6. Roast in the preheated oven for 20-25 minutes, or until the chicken is cooked through (internal temperature of 165°F/75°C) and the sweet potatoes are tender and golden brown.
7. If desired, broil for an additional 2-3 minutes at the end of cooking to brown the chicken and vegetables slightly.
8. Remove the baking sheet from the oven and let it cool for a few minutes.
9. Serve the Sheet Pan Buffalo Chicken with Sweet Potatoes and Green Beans hot, and enjoy your flavorful and satisfying meal!

This dish is perfect for a family dinner or a casual gathering, and it's sure to be a hit with its spicy buffalo chicken paired with sweet potatoes and crisp green beans.

Sheet Pan Rosemary Garlic Pork Chops with Brussels Sprouts and Apples

Ingredients:

For the pork chops:

- 4 bone-in pork chops
- 2 tablespoons olive oil
- 3 cloves garlic, minced
- 1 tablespoon fresh rosemary, chopped (or 1 teaspoon dried rosemary)
- Salt and black pepper, to taste

For the Brussels sprouts and apples:

- 1 pound Brussels sprouts, trimmed and halved
- 2 apples, cored and sliced
- 2 tablespoons olive oil
- 1 tablespoon balsamic vinegar
- 1 tablespoon honey
- Salt and black pepper, to taste
- 1 teaspoon fresh rosemary, chopped (or 1/2 teaspoon dried rosemary)

Instructions:

1. Preheat your oven to 400°F (200°C). Line a large baking sheet with parchment paper or aluminum foil for easy cleanup.
2. In a small bowl, mix together the olive oil, minced garlic, chopped rosemary, salt, and black pepper. Rub the mixture all over the pork chops, ensuring they are evenly coated. Set aside.
3. In a large bowl, toss together the halved Brussels sprouts and sliced apples with olive oil, balsamic vinegar, honey, salt, black pepper, and chopped rosemary until evenly coated.
4. Spread the Brussels sprouts and apples in a single layer on one side of the prepared baking sheet.
5. Place the seasoned pork chops on the other side of the baking sheet.

6. Roast in the preheated oven for 20-25 minutes, or until the pork chops reach an internal temperature of 145°F (63°C) and the Brussels sprouts are tender and caramelized.
7. If desired, broil for an additional 2-3 minutes at the end of cooking to brown the pork chops and vegetables slightly.
8. Remove the baking sheet from the oven and let it cool for a few minutes.
9. Serve the Sheet Pan Rosemary Garlic Pork Chops with Brussels Sprouts and Apples hot, and enjoy your delicious and comforting meal!

This dish is perfect for a cozy family dinner or a special occasion, and it's sure to impress with its savory pork chops paired with sweet and tangy Brussels sprouts and apples.

Sheet Pan Coconut Lime Shrimp with Pineapple and Peppers

Ingredients:

For the coconut lime shrimp:

- 1 pound large shrimp, peeled and deveined
- 1/4 cup coconut milk
- Zest and juice of 1 lime
- 2 cloves garlic, minced
- 1 tablespoon soy sauce
- 1 tablespoon honey
- 1 tablespoon olive oil
- Salt and black pepper, to taste
- Pinch of red pepper flakes (optional)
- Chopped cilantro, for garnish (optional)

For the pineapple and peppers:

- 1 small pineapple, peeled, cored, and cut into chunks
- 2 bell peppers (any color), cut into chunks
- 1 tablespoon olive oil
- Salt and black pepper, to taste
- 1 teaspoon chili powder (optional)

Instructions:

1. Preheat your oven to 400°F (200°C). Line a large baking sheet with parchment paper or aluminum foil for easy cleanup.
2. In a small bowl, whisk together the coconut milk, lime zest, lime juice, minced garlic, soy sauce, honey, olive oil, salt, black pepper, and red pepper flakes (if using) to make the marinade for the shrimp.
3. Place the peeled and deveined shrimp in a shallow dish or resealable plastic bag. Pour the marinade over the shrimp, making sure they are evenly coated. Let them marinate in the refrigerator for about 15-30 minutes.

4. In a large bowl, toss together the pineapple chunks and bell pepper chunks with olive oil, salt, black pepper, and chili powder (if using) until evenly coated.
5. Spread the marinated shrimp, pineapple chunks, and bell pepper chunks in a single layer on the prepared baking sheet, making sure they are not overcrowded.
6. Roast in the preheated oven for 10-12 minutes, or until the shrimp are pink and cooked through, and the pineapple and peppers are tender and slightly caramelized.
7. Remove the baking sheet from the oven and let it cool for a few minutes.
8. Optional: Garnish with chopped cilantro before serving.
9. Serve the Sheet Pan Coconut Lime Shrimp with Pineapple and Peppers hot, and enjoy your tropical and flavorful meal!

This dish is perfect for a quick weeknight dinner or a fun meal to enjoy with family and friends. The combination of coconut, lime, shrimp, pineapple, and peppers creates a deliciously vibrant and refreshing flavor profile.

Sheet Pan Mediterranean Chicken with Olives, Tomatoes, and Feta

Ingredients:

- 4 boneless, skinless chicken breasts
- 1 pint cherry tomatoes, halved
- 1/2 cup Kalamata olives, pitted
- 1/2 cup crumbled feta cheese
- 2 tablespoons olive oil
- 4 cloves garlic, minced
- 1 teaspoon dried oregano
- 1 teaspoon dried basil
- Salt and black pepper, to taste
- Fresh parsley, chopped, for garnish (optional)
- Lemon wedges, for serving (optional)

Instructions:

1. Preheat your oven to 400°F (200°C). Line a large baking sheet with parchment paper or aluminum foil for easy cleanup.
2. In a small bowl, whisk together the olive oil, minced garlic, dried oregano, dried basil, salt, and black pepper to make the marinade.
3. Place the chicken breasts in a shallow dish or resealable plastic bag. Pour the marinade over the chicken, making sure they are evenly coated. Let them marinate in the refrigerator for at least 30 minutes.
4. Arrange the marinated chicken breasts on the prepared baking sheet.
5. Scatter the halved cherry tomatoes and Kalamata olives around the chicken on the baking sheet.
6. Roast in the preheated oven for 20-25 minutes, or until the chicken is cooked through (internal temperature of 165°F/75°C) and the tomatoes are softened and juicy.
7. Remove the baking sheet from the oven and sprinkle the crumbled feta cheese over the chicken, tomatoes, and olives.
8. Optional: Broil for an additional 2-3 minutes at the end of cooking to brown the cheese slightly.
9. Remove from the oven and let it cool for a few minutes.
10. Garnish with chopped fresh parsley and serve hot with lemon wedges on the side, if desired.

11. Enjoy your delicious Sheet Pan Mediterranean Chicken with Olives, Tomatoes, and Feta!

This dish is perfect for a flavorful and easy weeknight dinner. The combination of juicy tomatoes, briny olives, tangy feta cheese, and aromatic herbs creates a mouthwatering Mediterranean-inspired meal that's sure to be a hit with your family and friends.

Sheet Pan Ranch Pork Chops with Potatoes and Broccoli

Ingredients:

For the ranch seasoning mix:

- 1 tablespoon dried parsley
- 1 teaspoon dried dill
- 1 teaspoon garlic powder
- 1 teaspoon onion powder
- 1/2 teaspoon dried chives
- 1/2 teaspoon dried thyme
- Salt and black pepper, to taste

For the pork chops, potatoes, and broccoli:

- 4 boneless pork chops
- 4 cups baby potatoes, halved or quartered
- 2 cups broccoli florets
- 2 tablespoons olive oil
- Ranch seasoning mix (from above)
- Salt and black pepper, to taste

Instructions:

1. Preheat your oven to 400°F (200°C). Line a large baking sheet with parchment paper or aluminum foil for easy cleanup.
2. In a small bowl, mix together all the ingredients for the ranch seasoning mix.
3. Place the pork chops, halved baby potatoes, and broccoli florets on the prepared baking sheet.
4. Drizzle the olive oil over the pork chops, potatoes, and broccoli.
5. Sprinkle the ranch seasoning mix evenly over everything on the baking sheet. Use your hands to rub the seasoning into the pork chops, potatoes, and broccoli, ensuring they are evenly coated. Season with additional salt and black pepper, if desired.

6. Arrange the pork chops, potatoes, and broccoli in a single layer on the baking sheet.
7. Roast in the preheated oven for 20-25 minutes, or until the pork chops are cooked through (internal temperature of 145°F/63°C) and the potatoes are tender and golden brown.
8. Remove the baking sheet from the oven and let it cool for a few minutes.
9. Serve the Sheet Pan Ranch Pork Chops with Potatoes and Broccoli hot, and enjoy your delicious and satisfying meal!

This dish is quick to prepare and requires minimal cleanup, making it perfect for busy nights. The ranch seasoning adds flavor to the pork chops and vegetables, creating a tasty and comforting meal that the whole family will love.

Sheet Pan BBQ Chicken with Corn on the Cob and Potatoes

Ingredients:

For the BBQ chicken:

- 4 bone-in, skin-on chicken thighs
- 1 cup barbecue sauce
- 2 tablespoons olive oil
- 2 cloves garlic, minced
- Salt and black pepper, to taste

For the corn on the cob and potatoes:

- 4 ears of corn, husked and halved
- 4 medium potatoes, cut into chunks
- 2 tablespoons olive oil
- Salt and black pepper, to taste
- Paprika, for sprinkling (optional)
- Chopped fresh parsley, for garnish (optional)

Instructions:

1. Preheat your oven to 400°F (200°C). Line a large baking sheet with parchment paper or aluminum foil for easy cleanup.
2. In a small bowl, mix together the barbecue sauce, olive oil, minced garlic, salt, and black pepper to make the marinade for the chicken.
3. Place the chicken thighs in a shallow dish or resealable plastic bag. Pour the barbecue sauce marinade over the chicken, making sure they are evenly coated. Let them marinate in the refrigerator for at least 30 minutes.
4. In a large bowl, toss together the halved ears of corn and potato chunks with olive oil, salt, and black pepper until evenly coated.
5. Spread the marinated chicken thighs, halved ears of corn, and potato chunks in a single layer on the prepared baking sheet.
6. Roast in the preheated oven for 30-35 minutes, or until the chicken is cooked through (internal temperature of 165°F/75°C) and the corn is tender and lightly browned.

7. If desired, sprinkle paprika over the corn for added flavor and color during the last few minutes of cooking.
8. Remove the baking sheet from the oven and let it cool for a few minutes.
9. Garnish with chopped fresh parsley before serving, if desired.
10. Serve the Sheet Pan BBQ Chicken with Corn on the Cob and Potatoes hot, and enjoy your delicious and satisfying meal!

This dish is perfect for a casual weeknight dinner or a summer barbecue. The barbecue sauce adds flavor to the chicken, while the roasted corn on the cob and potatoes are classic and comforting sides.

Sheet Pan Chili Lime Cod with Bell Peppers and Onions

Ingredients:

- 4 cod fillets (about 6 ounces each)
- 2 bell peppers, thinly sliced
- 1 large onion, thinly sliced
- 2 tablespoons olive oil
- Zest and juice of 2 limes
- 2 cloves garlic, minced
- 1 teaspoon chili powder
- 1/2 teaspoon ground cumin
- Salt and black pepper, to taste
- Fresh cilantro, chopped, for garnish (optional)
- Lime wedges, for serving (optional)

Instructions:

1. Preheat your oven to 400°F (200°C). Line a large baking sheet with parchment paper or aluminum foil for easy cleanup.
2. In a small bowl, whisk together the olive oil, lime zest, lime juice, minced garlic, chili powder, ground cumin, salt, and black pepper to make the marinade.
3. Place the cod fillets, bell pepper slices, and onion slices in a large bowl. Pour the marinade over them, tossing to coat evenly. Let them marinate for about 15-30 minutes.
4. Arrange the marinated cod fillets, bell pepper slices, and onion slices on the prepared baking sheet, making sure they are in a single layer.
5. Roast in the preheated oven for 12-15 minutes, or until the cod is opaque and flakes easily with a fork, and the bell peppers and onions are tender and slightly caramelized.
6. Remove the baking sheet from the oven and let it cool for a few minutes.
7. Optional: Garnish with chopped fresh cilantro before serving.
8. Serve the Sheet Pan Chili Lime Cod with Bell Peppers and Onions hot, and enjoy your zesty and delicious meal!

This dish is perfect for a quick weeknight dinner and is bursting with fresh flavors from the lime, chili powder, and cumin. The bell peppers and onions add color and texture, making it a well-rounded and satisfying meal. Serve it with rice or a side salad for a complete meal.

Sheet Pan Maple Balsamic Chicken with Brussels Sprouts and Squash

Ingredients:

For the maple balsamic marinade:

- 1/4 cup balsamic vinegar
- 2 tablespoons maple syrup
- 2 tablespoons olive oil
- 2 cloves garlic, minced
- 1 teaspoon Dijon mustard
- 1 teaspoon dried thyme
- Salt and black pepper, to taste

For the chicken and vegetables:

- 4 boneless, skinless chicken breasts
- 1 pound Brussels sprouts, trimmed and halved
- 1 small butternut squash, peeled, seeded, and cut into cubes
- 2 tablespoons olive oil
- Salt and black pepper, to taste
- Fresh parsley, chopped, for garnish (optional)

Instructions:

1. Preheat your oven to 400°F (200°C). Line a large baking sheet with parchment paper or aluminum foil for easy cleanup.
2. In a small bowl, whisk together the balsamic vinegar, maple syrup, olive oil, minced garlic, Dijon mustard, dried thyme, salt, and black pepper to make the marinade.
3. Place the chicken breasts in a shallow dish or resealable plastic bag. Pour half of the marinade over the chicken, reserving the other half for later. Let the chicken marinate in the refrigerator for at least 30 minutes.
4. In a large bowl, toss together the halved Brussels sprouts and cubed butternut squash with olive oil, salt, and black pepper until evenly coated.

5. Spread the marinated chicken breasts, Brussels sprouts, and butternut squash cubes in a single layer on the prepared baking sheet.
6. Roast in the preheated oven for 25-30 minutes, or until the chicken is cooked through (internal temperature of 165°F/75°C) and the vegetables are tender and caramelized, stirring the vegetables halfway through cooking.
7. Remove the baking sheet from the oven and let it cool for a few minutes.
8. Drizzle the remaining maple balsamic marinade over the cooked chicken and vegetables.
9. Optional: Garnish with chopped fresh parsley before serving.
10. Serve the Sheet Pan Maple Balsamic Chicken with Brussels Sprouts and Squash hot, and enjoy your sweet and savory meal!

This dish is perfect for a cozy fall or winter dinner and is sure to become a family favorite with its delicious combination of flavors.

Sheet Pan Teriyaki Tofu with Broccoli and Bell Peppers

Ingredients:

For the teriyaki sauce:

- 1/4 cup soy sauce
- 2 tablespoons water
- 2 tablespoons honey or maple syrup
- 1 tablespoon rice vinegar
- 1 clove garlic, minced
- 1 teaspoon grated ginger
- 1 tablespoon cornstarch
- 2 tablespoons water
- Sesame seeds, for garnish (optional)
- Sliced green onions, for garnish (optional)

For the tofu and vegetables:

- 1 block (14-16 ounces) extra-firm tofu, pressed and cubed
- 2 cups broccoli florets
- 2 bell peppers, thinly sliced
- 2 tablespoons olive oil
- Salt and black pepper, to taste

Instructions:

1. Preheat your oven to 400°F (200°C). Line a large baking sheet with parchment paper or aluminum foil for easy cleanup.
2. In a small saucepan, combine the soy sauce, water, honey or maple syrup, rice vinegar, minced garlic, and grated ginger. Heat over medium heat, stirring occasionally, until the mixture begins to simmer.
3. In a small bowl, mix together the cornstarch and water to make a slurry. Stir the slurry into the saucepan with the simmering sauce. Continue cooking, stirring constantly, until the sauce thickens. Remove from heat and set aside.

4. In a large bowl, toss together the cubed tofu, broccoli florets, and sliced bell peppers with olive oil, salt, and black pepper until evenly coated.
5. Spread the tofu, broccoli, and bell peppers in a single layer on the prepared baking sheet.
6. Bake in the preheated oven for 20-25 minutes, flipping the tofu halfway through cooking, until the tofu is golden and the vegetables are tender.
7. Once the tofu and vegetables are cooked, drizzle the teriyaki sauce over them and toss to coat evenly.
8. Optional: Sprinkle sesame seeds and sliced green onions over the tofu and vegetables before serving for extra flavor and garnish.
9. Serve the Sheet Pan Teriyaki Tofu with Broccoli and Bell Peppers hot, over rice or noodles if desired, and enjoy your delicious and nutritious meal!

This dish is perfect for a quick and healthy weeknight dinner and is packed with protein from the tofu and vitamins from the vegetables. The homemade teriyaki sauce adds a delicious sweet and savory flavor that everyone will love.

Sheet Pan Lemon Pepper Chicken with Green Beans and Potatoes

Ingredients:

For the lemon pepper chicken:

- 4 boneless, skinless chicken breasts
- 2 tablespoons olive oil
- Zest and juice of 1 lemon
- 2 cloves garlic, minced
- 1 teaspoon lemon pepper seasoning
- Salt and black pepper, to taste

For the green beans and potatoes:

- 1 pound baby potatoes, halved
- 1 pound green beans, trimmed
- 2 tablespoons olive oil
- Salt and black pepper, to taste
- 1 teaspoon garlic powder
- 1 teaspoon dried thyme

Instructions:

1. Preheat your oven to 400°F (200°C). Line a large baking sheet with parchment paper or aluminum foil for easy cleanup.
2. In a small bowl, whisk together the olive oil, lemon zest, lemon juice, minced garlic, lemon pepper seasoning, salt, and black pepper to make the marinade for the chicken.
3. Place the chicken breasts in a shallow dish or resealable plastic bag. Pour the marinade over the chicken, making sure they are evenly coated. Let them marinate in the refrigerator for at least 30 minutes.
4. In a large bowl, toss together the halved baby potatoes and trimmed green beans with olive oil, salt, black pepper, garlic powder, and dried thyme until evenly coated.

5. Spread the marinated chicken breasts, halved baby potatoes, and green beans in a single layer on the prepared baking sheet.
6. Roast in the preheated oven for 25-30 minutes, or until the chicken is cooked through (internal temperature of 165°F/75°C) and the potatoes are tender and golden brown.
7. If desired, broil for an additional 2-3 minutes at the end of cooking to brown the chicken and vegetables slightly.
8. Remove the baking sheet from the oven and let it cool for a few minutes.
9. Serve the Sheet Pan Lemon Pepper Chicken with Green Beans and Potatoes hot, and enjoy your delicious and satisfying meal!

This dish is quick to prepare and requires minimal cleanup, making it perfect for busy nights. The lemon pepper seasoning adds a bright and zesty flavor to the chicken, while the green beans and potatoes provide a hearty and nutritious side.

Sheet Pan Honey Sriracha Salmon with Snap Peas and Carrots

Ingredients:

For the honey sriracha marinade:

- 1/4 cup honey
- 2 tablespoons sriracha sauce
- 2 tablespoons soy sauce
- 1 tablespoon rice vinegar
- 2 cloves garlic, minced
- 1 teaspoon grated ginger
- Salt and black pepper, to taste

For the salmon and vegetables:

- 4 salmon fillets (about 6 ounces each), skin-on or skinless
- 8 ounces snap peas, trimmed
- 2 large carrots, peeled and sliced into thin strips (or use baby carrots)
- 2 tablespoons olive oil
- Salt and black pepper, to taste
- Sesame seeds, for garnish (optional)
- Sliced green onions, for garnish (optional)

Instructions:

1. Preheat your oven to 400°F (200°C). Line a large baking sheet with parchment paper or aluminum foil for easy cleanup.
2. In a small bowl, whisk together the honey, sriracha sauce, soy sauce, rice vinegar, minced garlic, grated ginger, salt, and black pepper to make the marinade.
3. Place the salmon fillets in a shallow dish or resealable plastic bag. Pour half of the marinade over the salmon, reserving the other half for later. Let the salmon marinate in the refrigerator for about 15-30 minutes.
4. In a large bowl, toss together the trimmed snap peas and sliced carrots with olive oil, salt, and black pepper until evenly coated.

5. Spread the marinated salmon fillets, snap peas, and carrots in a single layer on the prepared baking sheet.
6. Bake in the preheated oven for 12-15 minutes, or until the salmon is cooked through and flakes easily with a fork, and the vegetables are tender-crisp.
7. During the last few minutes of cooking, brush the reserved honey sriracha marinade over the salmon fillets for extra flavor.
8. Remove the baking sheet from the oven and let it cool for a few minutes.
9. Optional: Garnish the salmon with sesame seeds and sliced green onions before serving.
10. Serve the Sheet Pan Honey Sriracha Salmon with Snap Peas and Carrots hot, and enjoy your flavorful and nutritious meal!

This dish is perfect for a quick and healthy weeknight dinner. The sweet and spicy honey sriracha marinade pairs perfectly with the tender salmon and crisp vegetables, creating a delicious and satisfying meal.

Sheet Pan Caprese Chicken with Balsamic Glaze and Roasted Tomatoes

Ingredients:

For the chicken:

- 4 boneless, skinless chicken breasts
- 2 tablespoons olive oil
- Salt and black pepper, to taste
- 1 teaspoon Italian seasoning

For the Caprese topping:

- 2 large tomatoes, sliced
- 8 ounces fresh mozzarella cheese, sliced
- Fresh basil leaves
- Salt and black pepper, to taste
- Balsamic glaze, for drizzling

For the roasted tomatoes:

- 1 pint cherry tomatoes
- 2 tablespoons olive oil
- Salt and black pepper, to taste
- 2 cloves garlic, minced
- 1 teaspoon dried oregano

Instructions:

1. Preheat your oven to 400°F (200°C). Line a large baking sheet with parchment paper or aluminum foil for easy cleanup.
2. Place the chicken breasts on the prepared baking sheet. Drizzle with olive oil and season with salt, black pepper, and Italian seasoning.

3. Arrange the sliced tomatoes and mozzarella cheese over the chicken breasts. Top each chicken breast with fresh basil leaves. Season with salt and black pepper to taste.
4. In a small bowl, toss the cherry tomatoes with olive oil, minced garlic, dried oregano, salt, and black pepper. Spread the seasoned cherry tomatoes around the chicken on the baking sheet.
5. Roast in the preheated oven for 20-25 minutes, or until the chicken is cooked through (internal temperature of 165°F/75°C) and the cheese is melted and bubbly.
6. Remove the baking sheet from the oven and let it cool for a few minutes.
7. Drizzle the cooked chicken and roasted tomatoes with balsamic glaze just before serving.
8. Serve the Sheet Pan Caprese Chicken with Balsamic Glaze and Roasted Tomatoes hot, and enjoy the delicious combination of flavors!

This dish is perfect for a quick weeknight dinner or a special occasion. The juicy chicken topped with melted mozzarella, fresh tomatoes, and basil, drizzled with balsamic glaze, is sure to impress your family and friends.

Sheet Pan Mexican Street Corn Chicken with Potatoes and Peppers

Ingredients:

For the chicken:

- 4 boneless, skinless chicken breasts
- 2 tablespoons olive oil
- 2 cloves garlic, minced
- 1 teaspoon chili powder
- 1 teaspoon ground cumin
- 1 teaspoon paprika
- Salt and black pepper, to taste

For the corn:

- 4 ears of corn, husked and cut into thirds
- 2 tablespoons mayonnaise
- 1 tablespoon sour cream
- 1 tablespoon lime juice
- 1/4 cup cotija cheese, crumbled
- 1 tablespoon chopped fresh cilantro
- 1/2 teaspoon chili powder
- Lime wedges, for serving

For the potatoes and peppers:

- 1 pound baby potatoes, halved
- 2 bell peppers, sliced
- 2 tablespoons olive oil
- Salt and black pepper, to taste
- 1 teaspoon garlic powder
- 1 teaspoon smoked paprika
- Chopped fresh cilantro, for garnish (optional)

Instructions:

1. Preheat your oven to 400°F (200°C). Line a large baking sheet with parchment paper or aluminum foil for easy cleanup.
2. In a small bowl, mix together the olive oil, minced garlic, chili powder, ground cumin, paprika, salt, and black pepper to make the marinade for the chicken.
3. Place the chicken breasts in a shallow dish or resealable plastic bag. Pour the marinade over the chicken, making sure they are evenly coated. Let them marinate while you prepare the other ingredients.
4. In a separate bowl, mix together the mayonnaise, sour cream, and lime juice. Brush the corn pieces with the mixture, coating them evenly.
5. Place the corn on one side of the prepared baking sheet.
6. In the same bowl used for the corn mixture, add the halved baby potatoes, sliced bell peppers, olive oil, salt, black pepper, garlic powder, and smoked paprika. Toss until everything is well coated.
7. Spread the potato and pepper mixture on the other side of the baking sheet.
8. Place the marinated chicken breasts on top of the potato and pepper mixture.
9. Roast in the preheated oven for 25-30 minutes, or until the chicken is cooked through (internal temperature of 165°F/75°C) and the vegetables are tender, stirring the vegetables halfway through cooking.
10. While the chicken and vegetables are roasting, combine the crumbled cotija cheese, chopped cilantro, and chili powder in a small bowl.
11. Once the chicken is cooked through, remove the baking sheet from the oven.
12. Sprinkle the cotija cheese mixture over the roasted corn.
13. Garnish with chopped fresh cilantro, if desired.
14. Serve the Sheet Pan Mexican Street Corn Chicken with Potatoes and Peppers hot, with lime wedges on the side for squeezing over the chicken and corn.

This dish is bursting with flavors from the Mexican street corn and perfectly seasoned chicken, along with the roasted potatoes and peppers. It's a complete meal that's sure to be a hit with your family and friends!

Sheet Pan Lemon Garlic Herb Tilapia with Asparagus and Tomatoes

Ingredients:

For the tilapia:

- 4 tilapia fillets
- 2 tablespoons olive oil
- Zest and juice of 1 lemon
- 2 cloves garlic, minced
- 1 teaspoon dried Italian herbs (such as basil, oregano, and thyme)
- Salt and black pepper, to taste

For the vegetables:

- 1 pound asparagus, trimmed
- 1 pint cherry tomatoes, halved
- 2 tablespoons olive oil
- Salt and black pepper, to taste
- 2 cloves garlic, minced

Instructions:

1. Preheat your oven to 400°F (200°C). Line a large baking sheet with parchment paper or aluminum foil for easy cleanup.
2. In a small bowl, whisk together the olive oil, lemon zest, lemon juice, minced garlic, dried Italian herbs, salt, and black pepper to make the marinade for the tilapia.
3. Place the tilapia fillets in a shallow dish or resealable plastic bag. Pour the marinade over the tilapia, making sure they are evenly coated. Let them marinate while you prepare the vegetables.
4. Arrange the trimmed asparagus and halved cherry tomatoes on the prepared baking sheet. Drizzle with olive oil and sprinkle with minced garlic, salt, and black pepper. Toss to coat evenly.
5. Place the marinated tilapia fillets on top of the vegetables on the baking sheet.
6. Roast in the preheated oven for 12-15 minutes, or until the tilapia is cooked through and flakes easily with a fork, and the vegetables are tender.

7. Once cooked, remove the baking sheet from the oven.
8. Optional: Garnish the tilapia with additional lemon slices and chopped fresh herbs, such as parsley or basil.
9. Serve the Sheet Pan Lemon Garlic Herb Tilapia with Asparagus and Tomatoes hot, and enjoy your light and flavorful meal!

This dish is perfect for a quick weeknight dinner and is packed with fresh flavors from the lemon, garlic, and herbs. The tilapia becomes tender and flaky while baking alongside the vibrant asparagus and juicy cherry tomatoes, creating a delicious and nutritious meal.

Sheet Pan Ginger Soy Glazed Salmon with Broccoli and Rice

Ingredients:

For the ginger soy glaze:

- 1/4 cup soy sauce
- 2 tablespoons honey
- 1 tablespoon rice vinegar
- 1 tablespoon grated fresh ginger
- 2 cloves garlic, minced
- 1 tablespoon sesame oil
- 1 tablespoon cornstarch
- 2 tablespoons water

For the salmon and vegetables:

- 4 salmon fillets (about 6 ounces each)
- 1 head of broccoli, cut into florets
- 2 tablespoons olive oil
- Salt and black pepper, to taste

For serving:

- Cooked rice

Instructions:

1. Preheat your oven to 400°F (200°C). Line a large baking sheet with parchment paper or aluminum foil for easy cleanup.
2. In a small saucepan, combine the soy sauce, honey, rice vinegar, grated ginger, minced garlic, and sesame oil. Bring to a simmer over medium heat.

3. In a small bowl, mix together the cornstarch and water to make a slurry. Stir the slurry into the saucepan with the simmering sauce. Cook, stirring constantly, until the sauce thickens. Remove from heat and set aside.
4. Place the salmon fillets and broccoli florets on the prepared baking sheet. Drizzle with olive oil and season with salt and black pepper.
5. Brush the ginger soy glaze over the salmon fillets, reserving some for later.
6. Roast in the preheated oven for 12-15 minutes, or until the salmon is cooked through and flakes easily with a fork, and the broccoli is tender and slightly charred.
7. While the salmon and broccoli are roasting, cook the rice according to package instructions.
8. Once the salmon and broccoli are cooked, remove the baking sheet from the oven. Drizzle the remaining ginger soy glaze over the salmon and broccoli.
9. Serve the Sheet Pan Ginger Soy Glazed Salmon with Broccoli over cooked rice.
10. Enjoy your delicious and flavorful meal!

This dish is perfect for a quick and healthy weeknight dinner. The ginger soy glaze adds a wonderful umami flavor to the salmon, while the roasted broccoli adds freshness and crunch. Serve it over cooked rice for a complete and satisfying meal.

Sheet Pan Greek Lemon Chicken with Roasted Vegetables and Hummus

Ingredients:

For the Greek lemon chicken:

- 4 boneless, skinless chicken breasts
- 1/4 cup olive oil
- Zest and juice of 1 lemon
- 2 cloves garlic, minced
- 1 teaspoon dried oregano
- 1 teaspoon dried thyme
- 1/2 teaspoon dried rosemary
- Salt and black pepper, to taste

For the roasted vegetables:

- 1 large red bell pepper, sliced
- 1 large yellow bell pepper, sliced
- 1 red onion, sliced
- 1 zucchini, sliced
- 1 yellow squash, sliced
- 2 tablespoons olive oil
- Salt and black pepper, to taste
- 1 teaspoon dried oregano
- 1 teaspoon dried thyme

For serving:

- Hummus
- Lemon wedges
- Chopped fresh parsley, for garnish (optional)

Instructions:

1. Preheat your oven to 400°F (200°C). Line a large baking sheet with parchment paper or aluminum foil for easy cleanup.
2. In a small bowl, whisk together the olive oil, lemon zest, lemon juice, minced garlic, dried oregano, dried thyme, dried rosemary, salt, and black pepper to make the marinade for the chicken.
3. Place the chicken breasts in a shallow dish or resealable plastic bag. Pour the marinade over the chicken, making sure they are evenly coated. Let them marinate while you prepare the vegetables.
4. In a large bowl, toss together the sliced bell peppers, sliced red onion, sliced zucchini, and sliced yellow squash with olive oil, salt, black pepper, dried oregano, and dried thyme until evenly coated.
5. Spread the marinated chicken breasts and the seasoned vegetables in a single layer on the prepared baking sheet.
6. Roast in the preheated oven for 20-25 minutes, or until the chicken is cooked through (internal temperature of 165°F/75°C) and the vegetables are tender and slightly caramelized.
7. Once cooked, remove the baking sheet from the oven.
8. Serve the Sheet Pan Greek Lemon Chicken with Roasted Vegetables with a dollop of hummus on the side.
9. Garnish with lemon wedges and chopped fresh parsley, if desired.
10. Enjoy your delicious and satisfying meal!

This dish is bursting with Mediterranean flavors from the lemon, garlic, and herbs, and the roasted vegetables add a wonderful depth of flavor and texture. Serve it with hummus for a creamy and tangy accompaniment that complements the dish perfectly.

Sheet Pan Garlic Butter Pork Chops with Brussels Sprouts and Potatoes

Ingredients:

For the pork chops:

- 4 bone-in pork chops
- 4 tablespoons unsalted butter, melted
- 4 cloves garlic, minced
- 1 teaspoon dried thyme
- Salt and black pepper, to taste

For the vegetables:

- 1 pound Brussels sprouts, trimmed and halved
- 1 pound baby potatoes, halved
- 2 tablespoons olive oil
- Salt and black pepper, to taste
- 2 cloves garlic, minced
- 1 teaspoon dried rosemary

Instructions:

1. Preheat your oven to 400°F (200°C). Line a large baking sheet with parchment paper or aluminum foil for easy cleanup.
2. In a small bowl, mix together the melted butter, minced garlic, dried thyme, salt, and black pepper to make the garlic butter mixture for the pork chops.
3. Place the pork chops on the prepared baking sheet. Brush both sides of the pork chops with the garlic butter mixture.
4. In a large bowl, toss together the halved Brussels sprouts and baby potatoes with olive oil, salt, black pepper, minced garlic, and dried rosemary until evenly coated.
5. Spread the Brussels sprouts and potatoes around the pork chops on the baking sheet.
6. Roast in the preheated oven for 25-30 minutes, or until the pork chops are cooked through (internal temperature of 145°F/63°C) and the vegetables are tender and golden brown, stirring the vegetables halfway through cooking.

7. Once cooked, remove the baking sheet from the oven and let it cool for a few minutes.
8. Serve the Sheet Pan Garlic Butter Pork Chops with Brussels Sprouts and Potatoes hot, and enjoy your delicious and comforting meal!

This dish is hearty and satisfying, with tender pork chops infused with garlic butter flavor and perfectly roasted Brussels sprouts and potatoes. It's a complete meal that's easy to make and sure to be a hit with your family and friends.

Sheet Pan Honey Mustard Chicken with Brussels Sprouts and Carrots

Ingredients:

For the honey mustard chicken:

- 4 boneless, skinless chicken breasts
- 1/4 cup Dijon mustard
- 2 tablespoons honey
- 2 tablespoons olive oil
- 2 cloves garlic, minced
- 1 tablespoon apple cider vinegar
- Salt and black pepper, to taste

For the vegetables:

- 1 pound Brussels sprouts, trimmed and halved
- 1 pound carrots, peeled and sliced into sticks
- 2 tablespoons olive oil
- Salt and black pepper, to taste
- 1 teaspoon dried thyme

Instructions:

1. Preheat your oven to 400°F (200°C). Line a large baking sheet with parchment paper or aluminum foil for easy cleanup.
2. In a small bowl, whisk together the Dijon mustard, honey, olive oil, minced garlic, apple cider vinegar, salt, and black pepper to make the marinade for the chicken.
3. Place the chicken breasts in a shallow dish or resealable plastic bag. Pour the marinade over the chicken, making sure they are evenly coated. Let them marinate while you prepare the vegetables.
4. In a large bowl, toss together the halved Brussels sprouts and sliced carrots with olive oil, salt, black pepper, and dried thyme until evenly coated.
5. Spread the vegetables in a single layer on the prepared baking sheet.

6. Remove the chicken breasts from the marinade and place them on top of the vegetables on the baking sheet.
7. Roast in the preheated oven for 25-30 minutes, or until the chicken is cooked through (internal temperature of 165°F/75°C) and the vegetables are tender and caramelized, stirring the vegetables halfway through cooking.
8. Once cooked, remove the baking sheet from the oven and let it cool for a few minutes.
9. Serve the Sheet Pan Honey Mustard Chicken with Brussels Sprouts and Carrots hot, and enjoy your flavorful and nutritious meal!

This dish is perfect for a quick and healthy weeknight dinner. The tangy-sweet honey mustard marinade adds delicious flavor to the chicken, while the roasted Brussels sprouts and carrots provide a colorful and nutrient-rich side.

Sheet Pan Cajun Roasted Shrimp and Sausage with Peppers and Onions

Ingredients:

For the Cajun seasoning:

- 2 teaspoons paprika
- 1 teaspoon garlic powder
- 1 teaspoon onion powder
- 1 teaspoon dried thyme
- 1 teaspoon dried oregano
- 1/2 teaspoon cayenne pepper (adjust to taste)
- 1/2 teaspoon black pepper
- 1/2 teaspoon salt

For the shrimp and sausage:

- 1 pound large shrimp, peeled and deveined
- 12 ounces smoked sausage, sliced into rounds
- 2 bell peppers, sliced
- 1 large onion, sliced
- 2 tablespoons olive oil
- Cajun seasoning (from above), to taste
- Lemon wedges, for serving

Instructions:

1. Preheat your oven to 400°F (200°C). Line a large baking sheet with parchment paper or aluminum foil for easy cleanup.
2. In a small bowl, mix together all the ingredients for the Cajun seasoning.
3. In a large bowl, toss together the peeled and deveined shrimp, sliced smoked sausage, sliced bell peppers, and sliced onion with olive oil and Cajun seasoning until evenly coated.
4. Spread the shrimp, sausage, peppers, and onions in a single layer on the prepared baking sheet.

5. Roast in the preheated oven for 12-15 minutes, or until the shrimp are pink and opaque, and the sausage is heated through, stirring halfway through cooking.
6. Once cooked, remove the baking sheet from the oven and let it cool for a few minutes.
7. Serve the Sheet Pan Cajun Roasted Shrimp and Sausage with Peppers and Onions hot, with lemon wedges on the side for squeezing over the dish.
8. Enjoy your flavorful and delicious meal!

This dish is bursting with Cajun flavors and is quick and easy to make. The combination of juicy shrimp, smoky sausage, and tender roasted peppers and onions creates a satisfying meal that's perfect for any night of the week. Serve it with rice or crusty bread for a complete and hearty dinner.

Sheet Pan Pesto Salmon with Asparagus and Cherry Tomatoes

Ingredients:

For the pesto:

- 1 cup fresh basil leaves, packed
- 1/4 cup grated Parmesan cheese
- 1/4 cup pine nuts or walnuts
- 2 cloves garlic, minced
- 1/4 cup olive oil
- Salt and pepper to taste

For the salmon and vegetables:

- 4 salmon fillets (about 6 ounces each)
- 1 bunch asparagus, trimmed
- 1 pint cherry tomatoes, halved
- 2 tablespoons olive oil
- Salt and pepper to taste
- Lemon wedges for serving

Instructions:

1. Preheat your oven to 400°F (200°C). Line a large baking sheet with parchment paper or aluminum foil.
2. In a food processor, combine the basil, Parmesan cheese, pine nuts or walnuts, and garlic. Pulse until finely chopped.
3. With the food processor running, slowly drizzle in the olive oil until the pesto is smooth and well combined. Season with salt and pepper to taste. Set aside.
4. Place the salmon fillets on the prepared baking sheet. Spread a generous amount of pesto over each fillet.
5. In a large bowl, toss the trimmed asparagus and halved cherry tomatoes with olive oil, salt, and pepper until evenly coated.
6. Arrange the asparagus and cherry tomatoes around the salmon on the baking sheet.

7. Bake in the preheated oven for 12-15 minutes, or until the salmon is cooked through and flakes easily with a fork, and the vegetables are tender.
8. Once cooked, remove the baking sheet from the oven and let it cool for a few minutes.
9. Serve the Sheet Pan Pesto Salmon with Asparagus and Cherry Tomatoes hot, with lemon wedges on the side for squeezing over the salmon.
10. Enjoy your delicious and flavorful meal!

This dish is perfect for a quick and healthy weeknight dinner. The vibrant pesto adds a burst of flavor to the salmon, while the roasted asparagus and cherry tomatoes provide a fresh and colorful accompaniment. Serve it with a side of rice or crusty bread for a complete and satisfying meal.

Sheet Pan BBQ Ranch Pork Tenderloin with Potatoes and Green Beans

Ingredients:

For the pork tenderloin:

- 2 pork tenderloins (about 1 pound each)
- 1/2 cup BBQ sauce
- 2 tablespoons ranch seasoning mix
- Salt and black pepper, to taste

For the potatoes and green beans:

- 1 pound baby potatoes, halved
- 1 pound green beans, trimmed
- 2 tablespoons olive oil
- Salt and black pepper, to taste
- 1 teaspoon garlic powder
- 1 teaspoon onion powder

Instructions:

1. Preheat your oven to 400°F (200°C). Line a large baking sheet with parchment paper or aluminum foil for easy cleanup.
2. In a small bowl, mix together the BBQ sauce and ranch seasoning mix to make the marinade for the pork tenderloin.
3. Place the pork tenderloins on the prepared baking sheet. Season with salt and black pepper, then brush the BBQ ranch marinade over the tenderloins, making sure they are evenly coated.
4. In a large bowl, toss together the halved baby potatoes and trimmed green beans with olive oil, salt, black pepper, garlic powder, and onion powder until evenly coated.
5. Spread the seasoned potatoes and green beans around the pork tenderloins on the baking sheet.

6. Roast in the preheated oven for 25-30 minutes, or until the pork tenderloins reach an internal temperature of 145°F (63°C) and the vegetables are tender and slightly caramelized, stirring the vegetables halfway through cooking.
7. Once cooked, remove the baking sheet from the oven and let it rest for a few minutes.
8. Slice the pork tenderloins into medallions and serve with the roasted potatoes and green beans.
9. Enjoy your delicious Sheet Pan BBQ Ranch Pork Tenderloin with Potatoes and Green Beans!

This dish is packed with flavor from the BBQ ranch marinade, and the roasted potatoes and green beans complement the pork perfectly. It's a complete meal that's sure to be a hit with your family and friends.

Sheet Pan Lemon Herb Tofu with Broccoli and Cauliflower

Ingredients:

For the tofu:

- 1 block extra-firm tofu, pressed and drained
- 2 tablespoons olive oil
- Zest and juice of 1 lemon
- 2 cloves garlic, minced
- 1 teaspoon dried thyme
- 1 teaspoon dried rosemary
- Salt and black pepper, to taste

For the vegetables:

- 1 head of broccoli, cut into florets
- 1 head of cauliflower, cut into florets
- 2 tablespoons olive oil
- Salt and black pepper, to taste
- 1 teaspoon garlic powder
- 1 teaspoon dried thyme
- 1 teaspoon dried rosemary

Instructions:

1. Preheat your oven to 400°F (200°C). Line a large baking sheet with parchment paper or aluminum foil for easy cleanup.
2. Cut the pressed tofu into cubes and place them in a large bowl.
3. In a small bowl, whisk together the olive oil, lemon zest, lemon juice, minced garlic, dried thyme, dried rosemary, salt, and black pepper to make the marinade for the tofu.
4. Pour the marinade over the tofu cubes and toss until evenly coated. Let the tofu marinate while you prepare the vegetables.

5. In a large bowl, toss together the broccoli and cauliflower florets with olive oil, salt, black pepper, garlic powder, dried thyme, and dried rosemary until evenly coated.
6. Spread the marinated tofu cubes and seasoned broccoli and cauliflower florets in a single layer on the prepared baking sheet.
7. Roast in the preheated oven for 25-30 minutes, or until the tofu is golden and crisp around the edges, and the vegetables are tender and slightly caramelized, stirring halfway through cooking.
8. Once cooked, remove the baking sheet from the oven and let it cool for a few minutes.
9. Serve the Sheet Pan Lemon Herb Tofu with Broccoli and Cauliflower hot, and enjoy your flavorful and nutritious meal!

This dish is packed with protein from the tofu and plenty of vitamins and minerals from the broccoli and cauliflower. The lemon herb marinade adds a fresh and zesty flavor that pairs perfectly with the roasted vegetables. It's a simple and delicious vegetarian meal that's perfect for any day of the week.

Sheet Pan Moroccan Spiced Cod with Chickpeas and Bell Peppers

Ingredients:

For the Moroccan spice blend:

- 1 teaspoon ground cumin
- 1 teaspoon ground coriander
- 1 teaspoon smoked paprika
- 1/2 teaspoon ground cinnamon
- 1/2 teaspoon ground ginger
- 1/4 teaspoon ground turmeric
- Salt and black pepper, to taste

For the cod and vegetables:

- 4 cod fillets (about 6 ounces each)
- 1 can (15 ounces) chickpeas, drained and rinsed
- 2 bell peppers (any color), sliced
- 1 red onion, sliced
- 2 tablespoons olive oil
- Juice of 1 lemon
- 2 cloves garlic, minced
- Moroccan spice blend (from above)

Instructions:

1. Preheat your oven to 400°F (200°C). Line a large baking sheet with parchment paper or aluminum foil for easy cleanup.
2. In a small bowl, mix together all the spices to make the Moroccan spice blend. Set aside.
3. In a large bowl, toss together the drained and rinsed chickpeas, sliced bell peppers, sliced red onion, olive oil, lemon juice, minced garlic, and about 2 teaspoons of the Moroccan spice blend until everything is well coated.

4. Spread the chickpea and vegetable mixture in an even layer on the prepared baking sheet.
5. Place the cod fillets on top of the chickpea and vegetable mixture. Drizzle the cod fillets with a little olive oil and sprinkle with the remaining Moroccan spice blend.
6. Roast in the preheated oven for 15-20 minutes, or until the cod is opaque and flakes easily with a fork, and the vegetables are tender and slightly caramelized.
7. Once cooked, remove the baking sheet from the oven and let it cool for a few minutes.
8. Serve the Sheet Pan Moroccan Spiced Cod with Chickpeas and Bell Peppers hot, and enjoy your flavorful and nutritious meal!

This dish is bursting with Moroccan-inspired flavors and is packed with protein and fiber from the cod, chickpeas, and vegetables. It's a simple and delicious meal that's perfect for a quick weeknight dinner or a special occasion.

Sheet Pan Teriyaki Chicken with Pineapple and Snap Peas

Ingredients:

For the teriyaki sauce:

- 1/4 cup soy sauce
- 2 tablespoons honey
- 1 tablespoon rice vinegar
- 1 clove garlic, minced
- 1 teaspoon grated fresh ginger
- 1 tablespoon cornstarch
- 2 tablespoons water

For the chicken and vegetables:

- 4 boneless, skinless chicken breasts, cut into bite-sized pieces
- 1 cup pineapple chunks (fresh or canned)
- 1 cup snap peas, trimmed
- 1 bell pepper, sliced
- 2 tablespoons olive oil
- Salt and black pepper, to taste
- Cooked rice, for serving

Instructions:

1. Preheat your oven to 400°F (200°C). Line a large baking sheet with parchment paper or aluminum foil for easy cleanup.
2. In a small saucepan, combine the soy sauce, honey, rice vinegar, minced garlic, and grated ginger. Bring to a simmer over medium heat.
3. In a small bowl, mix together the cornstarch and water to make a slurry. Stir the slurry into the saucepan with the simmering sauce. Cook, stirring constantly, until the sauce thickens. Remove from heat and set aside.
4. In a large bowl, toss together the chicken pieces, pineapple chunks, snap peas, and sliced bell pepper with olive oil, salt, and black pepper until evenly coated.

5. Spread the chicken and vegetable mixture in a single layer on the prepared baking sheet.
6. Drizzle the teriyaki sauce over the chicken and vegetables, reserving some for later.
7. Roast in the preheated oven for 20-25 minutes, or until the chicken is cooked through and the vegetables are tender and slightly caramelized, stirring halfway through cooking.
8. Once cooked, remove the baking sheet from the oven and let it cool for a few minutes.
9. Serve the Sheet Pan Teriyaki Chicken with Pineapple and Snap Peas hot, over cooked rice, and drizzle with the reserved teriyaki sauce.
10. Enjoy your delicious and flavorful meal!

This dish is packed with sweet and savory flavors from the teriyaki sauce, juicy pineapple, and crisp snap peas. It's a quick and easy meal that's perfect for a busy weeknight dinner or a casual weekend meal with family and friends.

Sheet Pan Italian Herb Chicken with Roasted Vegetables and Potatoes

Ingredients:

For the Italian herb chicken:

- 4 boneless, skinless chicken breasts
- 2 tablespoons olive oil
- 2 cloves garlic, minced
- 1 tablespoon Italian seasoning
- 1 teaspoon dried basil
- 1 teaspoon dried oregano
- 1 teaspoon dried thyme
- Salt and black pepper, to taste

For the roasted vegetables and potatoes:

- 1 pound baby potatoes, halved
- 2 bell peppers (any color), sliced
- 1 red onion, sliced
- 2 tablespoons olive oil
- Salt and black pepper, to taste
- 1 teaspoon Italian seasoning
- 1/2 teaspoon garlic powder

Instructions:

1. Preheat your oven to 400°F (200°C). Line a large baking sheet with parchment paper or aluminum foil for easy cleanup.
2. In a small bowl, mix together the olive oil, minced garlic, Italian seasoning, dried basil, dried oregano, dried thyme, salt, and black pepper to make the marinade for the chicken.
3. Place the chicken breasts in a shallow dish or resealable plastic bag. Pour the marinade over the chicken, making sure they are evenly coated. Let them marinate while you prepare the vegetables and potatoes.

4. In a large bowl, toss together the halved baby potatoes, sliced bell peppers, and sliced red onion with olive oil, salt, black pepper, Italian seasoning, and garlic powder until evenly coated.
5. Spread the seasoned vegetables and potatoes in a single layer on the prepared baking sheet.
6. Remove the chicken breasts from the marinade and place them on top of the vegetables and potatoes on the baking sheet.
7. Roast in the preheated oven for 25-30 minutes, or until the chicken is cooked through (internal temperature of 165°F/75°C) and the vegetables are tender and slightly caramelized, stirring the vegetables halfway through cooking.
8. Once cooked, remove the baking sheet from the oven and let it cool for a few minutes.
9. Serve the Sheet Pan Italian Herb Chicken with Roasted Vegetables and Potatoes hot, and enjoy your comforting and flavorful meal!

This dish is bursting with Italian herb flavors and is a complete meal with protein from the chicken and plenty of vegetables and potatoes. It's perfect for a cozy weeknight dinner or a casual weekend meal with family and friends.

Sheet Pan Honey Garlic Glazed Pork Chops with Brussels Sprouts and Apples

Ingredients:

For the honey garlic glaze:

- 1/4 cup honey
- 2 tablespoons soy sauce
- 2 cloves garlic, minced
- 1 tablespoon apple cider vinegar
- 1 tablespoon olive oil
- Salt and black pepper, to taste

For the pork chops:

- 4 bone-in pork chops
- Salt and black pepper, to taste

For the Brussels sprouts, apples, and potatoes:

- 1 pound Brussels sprouts, trimmed and halved
- 2 apples, cored and sliced
- 1 pound baby potatoes, halved
- 2 tablespoons olive oil
- Salt and black pepper, to taste
- 1 teaspoon dried thyme
- 1 teaspoon dried rosemary

Instructions:

1. Preheat your oven to 400°F (200°C). Line a large baking sheet with parchment paper or aluminum foil for easy cleanup.
2. In a small bowl, whisk together the honey, soy sauce, minced garlic, apple cider vinegar, olive oil, salt, and black pepper to make the honey garlic glaze.

3. Season the pork chops with salt and black pepper on both sides.
4. Place the pork chops on the prepared baking sheet. Brush both sides of the pork chops with the honey garlic glaze, reserving some for later.
5. In a large bowl, toss together the trimmed and halved Brussels sprouts, sliced apples, halved baby potatoes, olive oil, salt, black pepper, dried thyme, and dried rosemary until evenly coated.
6. Spread the Brussels sprouts, apples, and potatoes around the pork chops on the baking sheet.
7. Roast in the preheated oven for 25-30 minutes, or until the pork chops are cooked through (internal temperature of 145°F/63°C) and the vegetables are tender and caramelized, stirring the vegetables halfway through cooking and brushing the pork chops with the remaining honey garlic glaze.
8. Once cooked, remove the baking sheet from the oven and let it cool for a few minutes.
9. Serve the Sheet Pan Honey Garlic Glazed Pork Chops with Brussels Sprouts and Apples hot, and enjoy your delicious and comforting meal!

This dish is perfect for a cozy fall dinner, with tender and juicy pork chops glazed with sweet and savory honey garlic sauce, and roasted Brussels sprouts, apples, and potatoes adding plenty of flavor and texture. It's a hearty and satisfying meal that's sure to be a hit with your family and friends.

Sheet Pan Lemon Pepper Shrimp with Broccoli and Potatoes

Ingredients:

For the lemon pepper shrimp:

- 1 pound large shrimp, peeled and deveined
- 2 tablespoons olive oil
- Zest and juice of 1 lemon
- 1 teaspoon lemon pepper seasoning
- Salt, to taste

For the broccoli and potatoes:

- 1 pound baby potatoes, halved
- 1 head of broccoli, cut into florets
- 2 tablespoons olive oil
- Salt and black pepper, to taste
- 1 teaspoon lemon pepper seasoning

Instructions:

1. Preheat your oven to 400°F (200°C). Line a large baking sheet with parchment paper or aluminum foil for easy cleanup.
2. In a large bowl, toss the peeled and deveined shrimp with olive oil, lemon zest, lemon juice, lemon pepper seasoning, and salt until evenly coated. Set aside.
3. In another large bowl, toss the halved baby potatoes and broccoli florets with olive oil, salt, black pepper, and lemon pepper seasoning until evenly coated.
4. Spread the seasoned potatoes and broccoli in a single layer on one side of the prepared baking sheet.
5. Spread the seasoned shrimp in a single layer on the other side of the baking sheet.
6. Roast in the preheated oven for 15-20 minutes, or until the shrimp are pink and opaque, and the potatoes are tender and lightly browned, stirring halfway through cooking.

7. Once cooked, remove the baking sheet from the oven and let it cool for a few minutes.
8. Serve the Sheet Pan Lemon Pepper Shrimp with Broccoli and Potatoes hot, and enjoy your quick and flavorful meal!

This dish is bursting with bright lemon flavor and the classic pairing of shrimp with broccoli and potatoes. It's simple to prepare and makes for a delicious and nutritious dinner option.

Sheet Pan Maple Dijon Chicken with Sweet Potatoes and Brussels Sprouts

Ingredients:

For the maple Dijon marinade:

- 1/4 cup maple syrup
- 2 tablespoons Dijon mustard
- 2 cloves garlic, minced
- 1 tablespoon olive oil
- Salt and black pepper, to taste

For the chicken and vegetables:

- 4 boneless, skinless chicken breasts
- 2 large sweet potatoes, peeled and diced
- 1 pound Brussels sprouts, trimmed and halved
- 2 tablespoons olive oil
- Salt and black pepper, to taste
- Chopped fresh parsley, for garnish (optional)

Instructions:

1. Preheat your oven to 400°F (200°C). Line a large baking sheet with parchment paper or aluminum foil for easy cleanup.
2. In a small bowl, whisk together the maple syrup, Dijon mustard, minced garlic, olive oil, salt, and black pepper to make the maple Dijon marinade.
3. Place the chicken breasts in a shallow dish or resealable plastic bag. Pour half of the marinade over the chicken, reserving the other half for later. Toss the chicken to coat evenly in the marinade. Let it marinate while you prepare the vegetables.
4. In a large bowl, toss together the diced sweet potatoes and halved Brussels sprouts with olive oil, salt, and black pepper until evenly coated.
5. Spread the sweet potatoes and Brussels sprouts in a single layer on the prepared baking sheet.

6. Place the marinated chicken breasts on top of the vegetables on the baking sheet.
7. Roast in the preheated oven for 25-30 minutes, or until the chicken is cooked through (internal temperature of 165°F/75°C) and the vegetables are tender and caramelized, stirring the vegetables halfway through cooking.
8. Once cooked, remove the baking sheet from the oven and let it cool for a few minutes.
9. Serve the Sheet Pan Maple Dijon Chicken with Sweet Potatoes and Brussels Sprouts hot, drizzled with the reserved maple Dijon marinade and garnished with chopped fresh parsley, if desired.

This dish is a perfect balance of sweet, tangy, and savory flavors, with tender and juicy chicken complemented by roasted sweet potatoes and Brussels sprouts. It's a satisfying and comforting meal that's easy to make and sure to be a hit with your family and friends.

Sheet Pan BBQ Ranch Salmon with Corn on the Cob and Potatoes

Ingredients:

For the BBQ ranch marinade:

- 1/4 cup BBQ sauce
- 2 tablespoons ranch seasoning mix
- 1 tablespoon olive oil
- 1 tablespoon honey

For the salmon and vegetables:

- 4 salmon fillets (about 6 ounces each)
- 4 ears of corn, husked and halved
- 1 pound baby potatoes, halved
- 2 tablespoons olive oil
- Salt and black pepper, to taste
- Chopped fresh parsley, for garnish (optional)

Instructions:

1. Preheat your oven to 400°F (200°C). Line a large baking sheet with parchment paper or aluminum foil for easy cleanup.
2. In a small bowl, whisk together the BBQ sauce, ranch seasoning mix, olive oil, and honey to make the BBQ ranch marinade.
3. Place the salmon fillets in a shallow dish or resealable plastic bag. Pour half of the marinade over the salmon, reserving the other half for later. Toss the salmon to coat evenly in the marinade.
4. In a large bowl, toss together the halved baby potatoes and halved ears of corn with olive oil, salt, and black pepper until evenly coated.
5. Spread the potatoes and corn in a single layer on the prepared baking sheet.
6. Place the marinated salmon fillets on top of the potatoes and corn on the baking sheet.

7. Roast in the preheated oven for 20-25 minutes, or until the salmon is cooked through (internal temperature of 145°F/63°C) and the potatoes are tender, stirring the vegetables halfway through cooking.
8. Once cooked, remove the baking sheet from the oven and let it cool for a few minutes.
9. Serve the Sheet Pan BBQ Ranch Salmon with Corn on the Cob and Potatoes hot, drizzled with the reserved BBQ ranch marinade and garnished with chopped fresh parsley, if desired.

This dish is a delightful combination of tangy BBQ sauce, zesty ranch seasoning, and succulent salmon, paired with tender roasted potatoes and sweet corn on the cob. It's a simple and satisfying meal that's sure to be a hit with your family and friends.

Sheet Pan Teriyaki Beef and Broccoli with Rice

Ingredients:

For the teriyaki sauce:

- 1/2 cup soy sauce
- 1/4 cup water
- 2 tablespoons honey
- 2 tablespoons brown sugar
- 1 tablespoon rice vinegar
- 2 cloves garlic, minced
- 1 teaspoon grated ginger
- 1 tablespoon cornstarch
- 2 tablespoons water

For the beef and broccoli:

- 1 pound flank steak, thinly sliced against the grain
- 1 head broccoli, cut into florets
- 2 tablespoons olive oil
- Salt and black pepper, to taste
- Cooked rice, for serving

Instructions:

1. Preheat your oven to 400°F (200°C). Line a large baking sheet with parchment paper or aluminum foil for easy cleanup.
2. In a small saucepan, combine the soy sauce, water, honey, brown sugar, rice vinegar, minced garlic, and grated ginger. Bring to a simmer over medium heat.
3. In a small bowl, mix together the cornstarch and water to make a slurry. Stir the slurry into the saucepan with the simmering sauce. Cook, stirring constantly, until the sauce thickens. Remove from heat and set aside.
4. In a large bowl, toss together the thinly sliced flank steak and broccoli florets with olive oil, salt, and black pepper until evenly coated.

5. Spread the beef and broccoli in a single layer on the prepared baking sheet.
6. Drizzle the teriyaki sauce over the beef and broccoli, reserving some for later.
7. Roast in the preheated oven for 12-15 minutes, or until the beef is cooked through and the broccoli is tender, stirring halfway through cooking and brushing the beef and broccoli with the reserved teriyaki sauce.
8. Once cooked, remove the baking sheet from the oven and let it cool for a few minutes.
9. Serve the Sheet Pan Teriyaki Beef and Broccoli with Rice hot, over cooked rice.

This dish is full of flavor from the homemade teriyaki sauce and the tender beef and broccoli. Serve it over cooked rice for a complete and satisfying meal that's sure to be a hit with your family and friends. Enjoy!

Sheet Pan Honey Mustard Veggie Tofu with Potatoes and Green Beans

Ingredients:

For the honey mustard marinade:

- 1/4 cup honey
- 2 tablespoons Dijon mustard
- 2 tablespoons olive oil
- 2 cloves garlic, minced
- Salt and black pepper, to taste

For the tofu and vegetables:

- 1 block extra-firm tofu, pressed and cubed
- 1 pound baby potatoes, halved
- 1 pound green beans, trimmed
- 2 tablespoons olive oil
- Salt and black pepper, to taste
- Chopped fresh parsley, for garnish (optional)

Instructions:

1. Preheat your oven to 400°F (200°C). Line a large baking sheet with parchment paper or aluminum foil for easy cleanup.
2. In a small bowl, whisk together the honey, Dijon mustard, olive oil, minced garlic, salt, and black pepper to make the honey mustard marinade.
3. Place the cubed tofu in a shallow dish or resealable plastic bag. Pour half of the marinade over the tofu, reserving the other half for later. Toss the tofu to coat evenly in the marinade.
4. In a large bowl, toss together the halved baby potatoes and trimmed green beans with olive oil, salt, and black pepper until evenly coated.
5. Spread the potatoes and green beans in a single layer on one side of the prepared baking sheet.
6. Spread the marinated tofu in a single layer on the other side of the baking sheet.

7. Roast in the preheated oven for 25-30 minutes, or until the tofu is golden and crispy, and the potatoes are tender and lightly browned, stirring halfway through cooking and brushing the tofu with the reserved honey mustard marinade.
8. Once cooked, remove the baking sheet from the oven and let it cool for a few minutes.
9. Serve the Sheet Pan Honey Mustard Veggie Tofu with Potatoes and Green Beans hot, garnished with chopped fresh parsley, if desired.

This dish is packed with flavor from the sweet and tangy honey mustard marinade, and the combination of crispy tofu, tender potatoes, and crunchy green beans makes it a satisfying and delicious meal. Enjoy!

www.ingramcontent.com/pod-product-compliance
Lightning Source LLC
LaVergne TN
LVHW081604060526
838201LV00054B/2079